Advance Praise for *Anattā: Heart of Wisdom*

"Michael Schauch has written a wonderful book. *Anattā* is a beautiful presentation of what the Buddhists call *shunyata,* usually translated as "emptiness," which means an ultimate Nonduality, another name for absolute Spirit. The "nonduality" part means that ultimate Reality is a perfect unity of all opposites—good vs. evil, up vs. down, left vs. right, legal vs. illegal, love vs. hate, and so on—what the Christian mystics call the *coincidentia oppositorum*—the coincidence of opposites. If you want to know why this is important, you've come to the right place—simply read this book. You'll learn the meaning of nonduality, and also why every single mystical tradition the world over maintains that ultimate Reality is nondual—which you'd think is something pretty important (it includes the opposites of you and Godhead, or you and Spirit, for example, which are often thought of as differentially contrasting). I highly recommend you buy this book and thus begin this most important quest for yourself."
—**KEN WILBER,** author of *Finding Radical Wholeness* and *A Brief History of Everything*

"Schauch writes about liberation—not through escape, but through intimacy with life as it is. By attuning to the wisdom of the heart, we begin to live from a place of connection rather than control."
—**SHARON SALZBERG,** author of *Lovingkindness* and *Real Life*

"Michael Schauch invites us on a profound journey beyond the 'conceptual mind' to the very 'language of the Heart.' Through this series of contemplative essays and stories, Schauch weaves together Tibetan and Japanese Buddhist insights to explore the sacred wisdom of 'non-self' and our deep interdependence with all living things. This book is a 'sword of light' for those ready to cut through the illusion of separateness and come home to the wisdom of Earth." —**JETSUNMA TENZIN PALMO**, author of *The Heroic Heart* and *Reflections on a Mountain Lake,* and Founder of the Dongyu Gatsal Ling Nunnery

"Schauch's collection of essays takes us on some astonishing adventures around the world. His well-crafted and layered prose shows remarkable inclusivity and sensitivity in spiritual, natural, and cognitive realms. Ultimately, *Anattā* feels like shelter in challenging times." —**BERNADETTE McDONALD**, author of *Alpine Rising* and *Freedom Climbers*

"Schauch's treasure of essays offers a wondrous glimpse of experiences that are beyond language and yet conveyed, ironically, through his beautiful words and gift of story. He illuminates possibilities for transcending the illusion of our separateness and guides us to tap into the vastness of our hearts and our interconnection with the natural world. Expansive and inviting, this little book is a trusted wellspring of wisdom and inspiration to return to time and again." —**SUSAN BAUER-WU, PhD, RN**, author of *A Future We Can Love* and *Leaves Falling Gently*

"*Anattā* is a small book, brimming with valuable insights and ageless wisdom. As a lifelong Buddhist practitioner and an experienced mountaineer, Schauch recounts incredible adventures and profound experiences in high, remote places. Shining through his gentle prose is the message of our interconnectedness with each other and with nature. In these difficult times, *Anattā* brings comfort, hope, and a guiding light." —**MARIA COFFEY**, author of *Explorers of the Infinite* and *Where the Mountain Casts Its Shadow*

Anattā

Heart of Wisdom

Anattā

Heart of Wisdom

MICHAEL SCHAUCH

HOHM PRESS
CHINO VALLEY, ARIZONA

Cover and interior design and layout by Jazmin Welch, fleck creative studio

Print ISBN: 978-1-963433-17-3
E-Book ISBN: 978-1-963433-18-0

Library of Congress Number: 2026937651

Printed and bound in the United States of America
First printing September 2026

Hohm Press
P.O. Box 4410
Chino Valley, AZ 86323
(800) 381-2700
hohmpress.com

For all my teachers.

To be.
To be with the sky and the air.
To be with the earth and the rock.
To be with the sun and the snow and the streams.
To be with the plants and the dirt and all living things.

As I am with them, they are with me.

Contents

Foreword

By Paula Arai

Wielding a "sword of light," Michael Schauch takes you by the heart as he skillfully crafts a wisdom-hued mandala of transformative relationships. Each essay connects us with places—from the Himalayan caves of Nepal to the Kamakura caves of Japan—and people—Chinese, Portuguese, Canadian, Tahltan, Newar, Tibetan, Japanese—guiding us together in a warming embrace.

Anattā (non-self) has an expansive perspective, offering us shelter from cynicism and despair even as it treads into the sobering realities of trauma and mental illness. Schauch's courageous and perceptive heart protects us from the corrosive effects of a world beleaguered by violence, injustice, and pain. He reminds us that there are realms of experience and dimensions of time that pulse through reality that we have access to when we choose "to soften...into the wisdom of the Heart." In Anattā, we can vicariously adventure to the heights of our planet and the depths of our spirits. Schauch takes us to summits of fearlessness and sacred sites where death nourishes life.

As a Buddhist scholar, I enjoyed the fluid connections between Tibetan and Japanese Buddhist insights. Not detained by explicating historical movements and philosophical influences, Schauch helps us feel how hearts from disparate regions of the

Buddhist world harmonize. We intuitively connect the 2,400-year-old bones in the "sky tombs" of Nepal with the graves of Adashino on the edge of the ancient capital of Kyoto. They both embody the sacredness with which people respect their deceased loved ones, a testament to the pulse that beats through all our hearts. We hear a chorus of spirits that animate our world as they echo through soaring mountains where contemporary Tibetan lamas, Zen masters, and Shingon master Kūkai have trekked.

One of Kūkai's most heralded wisdom insights is *hosshin seppō*, which means "Dharma Body preaches Dharma." Dharma Body (Dharmakāya) refers to the highest form of Dharma, which has traditionally been understood to be formless. The other two of the three Dharma bodies are the historical Buddha (*nirmanakāya*) and celestial Buddhas and Bodhisattvas (*sambhogakāya*). They take form. Kūkai teaches that the Dharma Body preaches a nondualistic twist that closes the distance between form and formlessness. Kūkai taught that seeing mist on a pond is to see the Dharma. Hearing birds sing is to hear the Dharma. Schauch's experiences with nature—the "ethereal glitter" of granite spires in Alaska, desert etchings "that whispered through the barrier of time" in Utah's Canyonlands, or a glowing campfire near his home in Squamish, BC—resonate with Kūkai's teachings.

I also hear echoes of thirteenth-century Zen master Dōgen in Schauch's stories. Dōgen himself echoes Kūkai. Dōgen too asserts a more nondualistic interpretation of a Buddhist teaching. He dissolves the distinction between sentient and nonsentient by reading the Nirvana Sutra passage, "All sentient beings have Buddha nature" as "All existents are Buddha nature." In harmony with Kūkai's view of Dharma Body as nature itself, Dōgen views Buddha nature as phenomenal reality, which encompasses all activities in nature. Both Kūkai and Dōgen dissolve the separation between form and formlessness, and conventional and ultimate reality. They live in a world where everything is precious; everything is worthy of the highest respect and deepest gratitude.

Schauch guides us into this world where mountains across continents are interconnected, where reified distinctions between self and non-self float away, and where our hearts come alive with wisdom.

One
Breath.
Inhale,
Exhale,
Remember.

Opening

Let come what comes. Let go what goes.
See what remains.

—Ramana Maharshi

EVER SINCE I WAS A CHILD, I've loved stories. I especially loved it when my mom read me bedtime stories. Books like Betty Waterton and Ann Blades's *A Salmon for Simon* or Farley Mowat's *Never Cry Wolf* created possibility. They connected me to different worlds and enriched the one I knew. They opened windows in my mind for new thoughts to enter and new dreams to awaken. There was nowhere they could not go, no language they could not speak, no truth they could not tell.

It is because of stories that we exist. Stories give us purpose. Stories give us life. They connect us. They challenge and inspire us to learn and grow. They awaken us to something greater than ourselves. Stories are embedded into our very core, as individuals, communities, and cultures. "You're never going to kill storytelling," says Margaret Atwood, "because it's built in the human plan. We come with it."[1]

But perhaps the greatest thing about stories is they can unlock a hidden language. This sacred wisdom within whispered to us even before we were born and will outlast us long after we're gone. We have not yet evolved enough to master this language. We fumble at the edges with our more conventional ways of communicating. And yet story is a language we already know, for we are made from it.

Throughout my childhood my mom shared many stories with me. But there is one that always stayed with me, a story from her own childhood. My mom grew up in a recovering post-Second World War Hong Kong. Born in Macau—once a quiet Portuguese island colony off the coast of China—to a Portuguese father and a Chinese mother, my mom moved with her family to Hong Kong when she was just an infant. Most of her childhood years were spent with her sister, six years her elder, and her mother who loved both her children dearly. The three of them lived in the flat of an old row house, which they shared in close quarters with three other families of relatives. Although times were trying and belongings meagre, she had a happy childhood.

That is until shortly before my mom's sixth birthday, when her mother unexpectedly died of tetanus. At first my mom had no idea what was happening. There was a gathering. Everyone had been overtaken by a deep sadness. My mom's sister cried endlessly. It was as if they all knew a terrible secret, one that was kept from her.

Then she saw her mother's body: cold, pale, and still. Lifeless. In that moment my mom understood. Her entire world crashed before her.

After the funeral, a shrine was created in the shared living room of their modest home—a few butter tea light candles, some sticks of incense, and their mother's photo in the centre of it. Before the shrine was a mattress where my mom would sleep with her sister.

One night as she slept, she felt a calming hand stroking her forehead. "I have to go now," said the soft voice above her. My mom sat upright. There before her was her mother in a white silken gown. Her mother then turned to the entrance door and passed through the shadow of the threshold. My mom called out to her. Nothing. She darted to the door, her tiny frame heaving the thick wooden beam barring the door and dropping it to the ground. She ran from their home barefoot into the open night in pursuit of her mother. Soon she reached the edge of a long terrace. To her right were a hundred stairs going up the hill, to her left a hundred stairs downhill. At the bottom of the stairs, she saw her mother before she vanished into the darkness. My mom called to her. But all was still and quiet. She collapsed at the top of the stairs, sobbing. Suddenly, she felt heavy arms wrap around her. One of the workers in the complex had heard her cries. He bundled my mom up and carried her back home.

There may be a thousand explanations as to what happened that night. But to this day my mom knows it was her mother. By honouring this knowledge, not repressing or dismissing it, her mother's love and kindness continued to be with her. To grow and flourish with her. And she with it. Her mother's love became a shield, giving my mom the courage and resilience to transcend the hardships she would ultimately face throughout her life. It is a love she would give to her own children. Her mother's spirit never left her.

And as it would happen, her mother's spirit passed to me too. Some might call it a guardian angel, or a protective deity. Whatever we name it, this transcendental presence has been a source of loving kindness for me from as far back as I can remember and has led to some of the most profound experiences of my life.

Much resides in the space where the conceptual mind cannot go. Like waves upon the ocean's surface, our thoughts may thrash and turn while beneath there is also a vast universe, fluent unto itself.

Whether we admit it or not, many of us have had experiences outside the realm of what our modern world would deem "normal." Often dismissed as paranormal phenomena, these extrasensory experiences likely appear as glimpses through the veil of our apparent reality when we least expect it—perhaps through a dream, a feeling or a vision, a memory, or some other manner of depth that reasoning cannot easily explain—even though at the time the experiences are as real as a glass of water sitting on the table before us.

And while our current context may condition us to easily dismiss such occurrences, these glimpses can be viewed as the awakening of a much deeper wisdom and world within us—one that has gently guided us from before we were born, and that has existed long before the languages of our modern world.

It is an ancient language. A sacred language. A language not of concepts but of Earth. It is the language of the Heart. The more we still ourselves, the clearer this language. The more we practise this stillness, the more we will hear it.

Although we may come with a universe of wisdom imprinted in us, we are also born to a blank canvas for our thoughts. We have a wide open space we can use to marvel at the world. In her book *The Philosophical Baby*, Alison Gopnik describes our youthful openness as "lantern consciousness."[2] As children we take in the world around us largely as it is. We are not yet set into thinking through layers, deeply rooted beliefs, modelled behaviours, or lived experiences. Because of this, our mind is least clouded during childhood. It's also when we are most lucidly aware of the sacred wisdom of Earth, as we often observe in children, who, like natural environmentalists, are quick to connect deeply with plants and animals. And it is why I believe my mom, at just shy of six, was able to clearly perceive and receive communication from her mother. There was nothing yet clouding her judgment of what was supposed to be "normal."

Early in life, our canvas fills in quickly. Studies show that during childhood what we experience, what we're told, and what we feel have the greatest impression and deepest imprint on us—so much so they can become entrenched into our very subconscious. Over time layers are built upon layers, until our canvas is filled with all kinds of thoughts, beliefs, and dualistic perceptions, potentially distorting or obscuring the sacred wisdom with which we are born. To open new space and free our mind, we must then work through the layers, softening and releasing the entrenched and often false perceptions—many of which we tend to grasp on to due to deep emotions, learned behaviours, or fear of losing ourselves.

When the late scientist and futurist James Lovelock introduced his Gaia hypothesis, it opened a new way for modern thinkers to look at life on Earth. Lovelock theorized we exist not as individual parts unto ourselves but as part of a single greater unified Self. As he wrote, "The most important thing we can do to undo the harm we have done is to fix firmly in our minds the thought: *the Earth is alive.*"[3]

In his celebrated works, Lovelock advocates that not only is Earth alive, but it is an individual organism that has evolved over billions of years—and the "entire range of living matter on Earth from whales to viruses and from oaks to algae could be regarded as constituting a single living entity capable of maintaining the Earth's atmosphere to suit its overall needs and endowed with faculties and powers far beyond those of its constituent parts."[4]

Endowed with faculties and powers far beyond those of its constituent parts.

Perhaps then it is not about us trying to change the world but to liberate our inner awareness enough to understand we are small parts of something far greater and far more intelligent than we know.

If, for example, we humans were as old as Earth, and held the wisdom of a billion years of evolution, what would be our purpose? What would be our language? Would we not exist to simply be? Would our language not be the sound of the waters upon the shore? The chorus of birds free in flight? The whisper of winds through the bristled treetops, or the slow spread of lichen upon the stone? Or the great silence of nature's unabated stillness?

Would not all distinction dissolve as a decaying leaf into the earth, blurring boundaries and lines of beginning and end?

Where would memory reside? Where would consciousness reside?

For more than a thousand years, Tibetan Buddhists have used the term *tendrel* to describe the complex existence of which we are a part. *Ten* means "to depend," and *drel* means "connection" or "relationship." *Tendrel* translates as "dependent connection," or "interdependence."[5] In other words, nothing exists by itself, for everything arises and exists because of everything else, and hence is intrinsically and wholistically one. Like a web made up of billions upon billions of strands, nothing remains still; the smallest vibration echoes through one entire unified system expanding outward while creating and shaping countless new vibrations along the way, which simultaneously return to and change each vibration's source. We, like all else, are part of one ever-enduring, ever-evolving creation. An interconnected consciousness spanning both time and space.

The Buddhist view of interdependence understands that our true self exists beyond the individual, and the belief in the illusion of the individual as our true self is the source of suffering on Earth. The more we liberate our minds to our interconnectedness, the more we will begin to make choices to heal our sufferings and the sufferings of others. In other words, the more we understand our connection to all that is, the more we can begin to transform our deepest hurt into wisdom.

To understand the wisdom of interdependence is to soften deeply into ourselves, beyond the deepest depths of the *skandhas*—"roughly, the physical body, sensation-perception, emotion-impulse, lower cognition, and higher cognition."[6] In other words, beyond every layer, every part, and every idea of who and what we think we are. Even beyond the one who is perceiving. Beyond what in our lives may have come before. Beyond what in our lives may yet come to be.

Tibetan Lama Chögyam Trungpa Rinpoche spoke of invoking the *drala*, which is to "connect the wisdom of our own inner being with the power of things as they are." According to Trungpa Rinpoche, it is human tendency to "shut any vastness or possibilities of deeper perception out of our hearts by fixating on our own interpretation of phenomena. But it is possible to go beyond personal interpretation...We always have a choice: We can limit our perception so that we close off vastness, or we can allow vastness to touch us."[7]

We can allow vastness to touch us.

In Sanskrit, this deeper wisdom is called *prajñā*—described as the "antidote to ignorance and the means of liberating the mind from suffering."[8] It is a divine wisdom that illuminates the unified Truth and cuts through all other untruth like a sword of light. A unified wisdom. An Earth wisdom. A Heart wisdom. By allowing the vastness of the outside to connect with the vastness of our heart, we can begin to transcend the illusion or false perception of our separateness as the centre of our own experience and world.

When Gautama Buddha was asked by his disciple Ananda, "What is all this for? What have you gained from all this meditation?" Buddha replied simply: "Nothing. But I have lost a lot." Buddha had softened through the untold layers of self, recognizing the true nature of all phenomena, and thereby opened into the Truth of all that is.

The great luminaries have been educating us on the Truth of our existence for thousands of years, just not in the language our relatively young thinking minds would typically understand. "Reason," as American philosopher Ken Wilber observes, "cannot grasp the essence of absolute reality, and when it tries, it generates only dualistic incompatibilities."[9] In other words, we cannot *think* our way to the Truth of our essence. The more we try, the further away we move from it. Since our rational minds—and therefore conventional language—have not yet evolved enough to fully understand this sacred Truth, luminaries have instead spoken through the tongue of story and metaphor.

For example, one of the oldest and most significant Bodhisattvas—Manjushri, who is the embodiment of enlightenment and transcendent wisdom—is depicted wielding a flaming sword, a sword of light, symbolizing the Truth of existence cutting through the duality and untruth of the illusion of an independent self. Manjushri is also usually atop a lion, representing the taming of our dualistic mind (overcoming false perception).

In Christian faith, Archangel Saint Michael—widely considered the foremost messenger of God (the root word of "angel" is messenger)—is also portrayed wielding a sword of light and overcoming the devil (the light of God, or Truth, freeing the mind of illusion or false perceptions).

"They live in wisdom who see themselves in all and all in them," said Krishna, a divine representation of the Truth of all that exists, in what is perhaps the most prominent and influential of Hindu scriptures, the Bhagavad Gita.

In 2013, and again in 2014, my wife Chantal and I spent several days in the Tahltan Highlands in Northern British Columbia with members of the Tahltan First Nation, learning from and connecting with one of the last naturally intact places on Earth. Together we traversed a hundred kilometres—crossing untold creeks and streams, winding through many valleys, traversing over mountain ranges and glaciers. During our time on the land, I frequently heard the expression, "All my relations," which I've come to understand as the sacred wisdom and unified existence of all that is—including all who live and all who have lived, and all the phenomena of Earth from the smallest of grains to the greatest of mountains. This phrase is indeed well known across all First Nations and Indigenous Peoples throughout North America.

By opening ourselves to our true nature, and indeed the true nature of all that is, we align ourselves with the wisdom of Earth—a sacred wisdom that has evolved for billions of years and continues to evolve.

For millennia, Buddhists have spoken about the extrasensory abilities of aligning with this wisdom (though more as a "side effect" of practice versus something to work toward)—evoking the opening of psychic powers, knowledge and memory of past lives, telepathy, time travel, clairvoyance, the realization of the astral body from physical body, and even levitation. And communicating with those who have passed.

What may not be "normal" to many is normal to those who ascribe to the ancient wisdoms and languages forgotten by our modern world. As Jared Diamond observes in *The World Until Yesterday*, much of what we in the modern world consider normal has only been considered as such for a blink of an eye. Prior to this, "until virtually yesterday," as Diamond notes, traditional societies—our ancestors—lived an altogether different way for tens of thousands of years.[10]

Or as my dear friend Brent once said, "Those moving about in crazy ways only appear to be crazy until you can hear the music."

At some point in our life a line is drawn between what is real and what is not. But who draws this line? Who decides what is real and what is not? Who decides where the conceptual language of the mind ends and the boundless language of the Heart begins? And why is what we are unable to easily measure or perceive—like the depth of the ocean beneath the waves—dismissed and suppressed as illusory?

Even now we struggle to grapple with what consciousness is. We think we know who we are, and yet we know we are not what we can physically observe or measure. Just as we have evolved to understand the complexity and intelligence of a unified living forest beyond a cluster of individual trees, or how the various ecosystems and their myriad species coexist, we continue to expand our awareness about the health of our bodies and minds and their complex union with all that is. As Gabor Maté declares in *The Myth of Normal*, "If we want a clear and accurate view of human health, we will have to broaden our understanding of 'bodymind' to include the myriad roles that *other* minds and *other* bodies play in shaping our wellbeing, indeed our very sense of self. Unity, it turns out, extends well beyond the unitary individual."[11]

Unity extends well beyond the unitary individual.

If we soften our minds to see Earth as a singular living organism, with its own unique consciousness—not defined by our limited and fledgling understanding of what consciousness is, nor one we have modelled after ourselves but one that has existed and evolved over a time span far beyond our ability to fathom—what is to say we are not simply microscopic parts of a unified whole? Microbes of a wholistic being with a wholistic consciousness—like countless branches of streams flowing into one great ocean.

In his final work, *Man and His Symbols*, Carl Jung observes, "As scientific understanding has grown, so our world has become dehumanized. Man feels himself isolated in the cosmos, because he is no longer involved in nature and has lost his emotional 'unconscious identity' with natural phenomena. No voices now speak to man from stones, plants, and animals, nor does he speak to them believing they can hear. His contact with nature has gone, and with it has gone the profound emotional energy that this symbolic connection supplied."[12]

We do not need to look far to see how the loss or suppression of understanding the sacred wisdom of Earth has impacted all who inhabit it. The deep wounds we have fostered and perpetuated within ourselves and each other. The deep wounds we have inflicted upon Earth at large. We know what happens to our bodies and minds when we suppress anything—the blockages, inflammation, diseases, illnesses, and traumas that take root and propagate. Since we are interdependent and innately part of Earth, we are now witnessing and experiencing this suffering on an augmented global scale as Earth adapts and responds. After all, as Lovelock observed, "Nature favors those organisms which leave the environment in better shape for their progeny to survive."[13]

Never has there been a more important time to awaken and align ourselves with the sacred wisdom of our Earth, the wisdom of the Heart—one that is already finely attuned within us, for it *is* us. By speaking and being this sacred Truth, we honour it. By honouring it, we heal. By healing, we exist.

This is not a book about trying to solve the climate crisis or resolve mental traumas. Nor is it a self-help book, or a guide to live a better life or improve your relationships with others or your relationship with yourself—although the stories that follow may result in positive changes in these areas. It is a book for those who wish to take the critical step to soften into and connect with the unspoken language of the Heart.

Much of what is presented here surfaced from extensive meditation and the personal experiences and insights that arose as a result. Some messages came to me through various forms of immersive mindfulness techniques—such as deep breathwork, yoga, and hypnotherapy, or by spending time in nature and the mountains, or simply by allowing myself to be deeply still and present.

Some openings arose due to place—such as sacred valleys isolated from our modern civilization and more closely connected to the energy of Earth—in the Himalaya, or in the mountains of Northern British Columbia. For millennia lamas and yogis have recognized such places as having a clearer link between our Heart wisdom and the wisdom of Earth. A frequency with less static, a veil that is less opaque, where there are fewer disturbances and our mind can more easily meditate and soften into the essence of its true nature. Other openings occurred in places such as Lumbini, Nepal, where Gautama Buddha was born—places imbued with the deep emotional and energetic imprints of many others over thousands of years.

I've heard stories of others having similar experiences—tapping into the wisdom of the Heart, the wisdom of Earth, through the use of psychedelics. Listening to these stories, there is a clear recurring theme: They all speak of witnessing and experiencing in some form a deeper Truth beyond the self, cutting through our own false perceptions and self-constructs and self-practised limitations.

While there may be similarities, I do feel compelled to say I have never used any form of psychedelics, and therefore do not feel equipped to elaborate on them. Although I will say this: While many psychedelics are derived naturally from Earth, and hence carry with them its sacred wisdom, I do feel there is value in *choosing* to soften oneself into the wisdom of the Heart, rather than arriving there by way of substances designed to alter our state of consciousness. It's akin to climbing a mountain versus suddenly and momentarily appearing on its summit to see the whole view. There is value in the climb.

After all, the practice is the Way.

The insights that follow are presented through six contemplative essays and poetry, and through stories, as I believe stories can speak the wisdom of the Heart, as I learned in childhood and from my mom. If possible, I suggest you read the following essays in a quiet place. Take your time with them. They are meant to be revisited.

Since I have long been a student of Buddhism, I've drawn on this ancient study throughout the book to help support and garner greater insight into what the conceptual mind cannot easily understand.

I hope this book gives you something that awakens and harmonizes with the sacred voice within you, perhaps opening a new doorway or reaffirming what you have long already known to be true. May this alignment help soften the layers of the mind and heart, so you may open, act, liberate, and create from the vast and eternal wisdom within—a practice so drastically needed and not done nearly enough.

In the words of Hermann Hesse: "...mountain and river, tree and leaf, root and blossom, every form in nature, has a pre-image inside us; it originates from the soul, whose nature is eternity, whose nature we don't know but is generally revealed to us as the power of love and creativity."[14]

May we come to realize the true essence of ourselves. Of our mind, which is actually "no mind," or rather universal mind: an interconnected consciousness rooted in the language of the Heart.

May we learn to remember and create anew what has been with us all along: the sacred wisdom of Earth, a living being wise beyond our understanding, and yet which has instilled within us that wisdom so we may exist with the unified greatness, grace, and love with all that is.

May there be virtue.

MICHAEL SCHAUCH
Skwxwú7mesh-ulh Temíxw (Squamish, BC, Canada)

Before me was a great tree, which stretched toward the sky like a mountain. Its bark was crevassed and as hard as stone. Its leaves glowed soft and green as a sapling. It was the Tree of All Life.

As I stood before the tree, I noticed fine particles floating away from its bark and disappearing into nothingness. I placed my hand on the Tree of All Life and asked how we can stop this from happening.

The great tree replied, “Speak the Truth. Be the Truth. Speaking and being the Truth is water to my roots and sun to my leaves.”

Bones

If you could see the bones from your past lives, they would be piled higher than Chomolungma.

—Tibetan monk

IT WASN'T JUST A CAVE. It was a tomb.

A shadow of fear crept through my mind as the faint light from my head torch swept across the cavern floor. What I saw should have repulsed me. But something drew me deeper into the darkness. Hundreds, perhaps thousands, of human bones—skulls, spinal cords, ribs, and femurs—were scattered and heaped in the pitch black.

My Sherpa companion Ngawang remained close to the cavern's exit, his usual joyful disposition replaced by the look of seeing a ghost. Or angering one. Meanwhile, young Umang was busy sorting through the various skeletal remains like a student in an anatomy class.

Behind Umang the cavern wall glittered in the light of my torch. It was layered with some sort of thick mineralized shell, a prehistoric coral-like crystalline that reflected our lamps in dazzling colour.

Cold rock touched my lungs under shallow breath. An emptiness older than time lingered in the dark. The air was as still as the bones. We weren't supposed to be in here.

After all, I thought I was coming to the Himalaya to climb a mountain, one I'd only identified through a friend's photograph. It was a mysterious pyramidal peak that had drawn me to one of the most far-flung and isolated corners in the upper Manang district of northern Nepal. The pyramid mountain called to me like a beacon. I yearned to feel it, to experience it. To be a part of it, even if only for a moment. And to a mountaineering fanatic with a dream of climbing in the Himalaya since childhood, it was perfect.

But the quest that took nearly two decades to materialize, bringing us so tantalizingly close to the mountain, had ended. We'd been thwarted by a severe snowstorm at an elevation of five thousand metres, and the mule carrying my climbing gear had run away. There was nothing left to do but turn back. Some part of me inside, a deep void, felt like a failure. As though a long-held vision for my life, and thus my very identity, had somehow been swallowed by a bottomless crevasse. I felt lost in my heart.

And yet seeing the cave high up in the cliffside ignited something new, some new curiosity. The depthlessness called to me. *What is this force that pulls me into it?* I craned my neck, feeling all my thoughts bend into the black hole. Before its entrance were the remnants of a man-made wall, something of a forgotten age. A wall made to keep something out...or something in?

I felt my backpack slide off one shoulder and drop to the ground and, as if possessed by some unseen force, I began scaling the cliff face. Ngawang and Umang climbed with me while my wife Chantal and the rest of our team watched us from the valley below. We scrambled up craggy rock in tandem, carefully testing each hold. The stone was loose and crumbly, and some of the holds dislodged at our touch, bouncing down to the valley floor some fifty metres below.

Keep going, Mike. You've got this.

Before long we found ourselves staring into the void; an icy current touched our faces. Then, one by one, we flicked on our head torches and entered the abyss through a passageway.

We crawled and clambered single file in silence, making our way deeper into the mountain. Parts of the tunnel were so narrow we could barely squeeze our bodies through. Fine, ash-like sand lining the walls gave way as we passed. Bat droppings were everywhere. It didn't look like anyone had been in there in a long, long time.

And then we reached the end. And with it the tomb.

Umang was still immersed in the bones. He turned to me with an ear-to-ear grin, holding up to his face a fully intact jawbone, some of its teeth still affixed. When looking through my footage later, I realized the young Sherpa could fit his entire face inside of it.

The glittering wall entranced me. I leaned into it. Flashes of colour awakened, seeming to arouse at the light of my torch. I tapped my knuckles against the wall. A muffled echo answered from behind. The whole thing was a shell. A living phenomenon of the cave. I wondered if the dead had given the cave life. Bones of the earth.

The eeriness of it all was getting to me. We slowly backed away from the burial, trying not to disturb anything else, and retreated down the passageway.

When we reached the nearby settlement, we asked as many of the locals as we could about the bones. But no one knew anything about any bones in the cave. Not even a seventy-year-old woman who was the oldest person we could find in the village. A new curiosity began to grow in my mind.

I'd left the cave, but it had already become a part of me. *Who were these people? What was their story? Why were they buried so deep within the mountain?* I wondered if the cave wasn't only a tomb, a resting place for the dead. Perhaps it had been sanctified as some sort of passage, a doorway from which the dead had passed through the end of one life into the next.

I'd read about such a place in the *Bardo Thodol*, otherwise known as *The Tibetan Book of the Dead*. It is called the *bardo*. A gap. A state of transition between death and rebirth—between who we were and who we become.

While many understand reincarnation as death and rebirth from lifetime to lifetime, Tibetan Buddhists also believe we experience many cycles of death and rebirth in one lifetime, since parts of us are continuously dying and parts of us are being reborn—ever changing, never stagnant. We are not the same person we were when we were born. Nor are we the person we were ten years ago, five years ago, or even last week. And who we are becoming is not who we are today. As we navigate these mindscapes, we are (often unknowingly) entering in and out of the bardos of life. Being in the bardo can be confusing.

Tibetan Lama Chögyam Trungpa Rinpoche spoke of the bardo as "an island in the midst of a lake."[15] We've abandoned one shore, existing now in memory; and the shore ahead of us is unknown, still too far away to see. We are left in an unfamiliar expanse. It is here, however, that we may choose *who* we become. What are we grasping for? What no longer serves us? What can we simply let be? Where can we soften? And what space are we able to expand into?

Do not get lost in the bardo, the Tibetans warn. *Do not get lost in the bardo.* In other words, do not move forward into the unknown while grasping for the myriad stories born of our minds. In this way, confusion and stress set in by trying to move through a doorway between our attachments and our becoming. We lose ourselves in a vicious cycle that is hard to escape, and the energy we feed into sustaining our illusions drains our life force, perpetuating the suffering that binds us. Some of us spend years or even lifetimes in the bardo.

What keeps us tethered to the past or the future is what we choose to keep within us. We create our own bardo by what we cling to.

I've learned that while moving through the bardo may be both frightening and confusing—as though we are crawling directionless through a dark cave or struggling to climb out of a pit of despair—it is the path of liberation from our self. There is life in death. We move forward by letting parts of ourselves die—be it beliefs, expectations, experiences, parts of our identity, or emotional traumas, which in turn plants the seeds for rebirth. "We must have felt what it is to die," observes Edward Dantes in *The Count of Monte Cristo*, "that we may appreciate the enjoyments of life."[16]

As we shed new layers, akin to a snake shedding its skin, we enter a process of unmasking. Trungpa Rinpoche described this as "an unmasking of everything that we try to hide behind, such as the philosophy we have developed."[17] We unearth new masks and are born into deeper understandings of ourselves, which we can then learn to shed as well.

And through every rebirth we turn confusion into wisdom, hurt into compassion, and we free ourselves bit by bit to the depths of what can be.

Not long after arriving back home in Canada, I spotted the latest edition of *National Geographic* on a magazine rack. Its cover headline jumped at me: "Nepal's Secret Caves." I dove into the feature at once. The article detailed the work of Mark Aldenderfer, a National Geographic explorer and professor of anthropology who'd been researching ancient sky caves—or "sky tombs," as he calls them—in the Himalaya a few valleys west of where we had been. We promptly reached out to Mark and gave him the coordinates of our bone cave. About a year later, the veteran anthropologist returned to Nepal with his team.

Several months later I received a note from Mark.

Inside the cave were the remains of twenty-three individuals and their animals. They'd been placed there nearly 2,400 years ago.

They were early explorers from the north, from what is now Tibet. They were self-supported, weaving their own clothes and carving their own tools and utensils out of wood and other local materials. Something compelled them to leave the Tibetan plateau and travel high into the mountains, traversing the great Himalayan passes. They navigated the unforgiving vertical landscapes, using some of the same routes and passages we had used.

But then something ill-fated happened, likely an unforeseen epidemic or disease. The sickness was impartial, spreading through their community and wiping out entire families. Many died prematurely, some of them in their early teenage years. The surviving members buried their dead deep in the cliffside cave.

Perhaps Mark's most intriguing find were the small firebrands placed around the dead. To the inexperienced eye they were nothing more than charred wooden sticks. Upon closer inspection, however, Mark had identified finely detailed images pressed into the wood—human figurines wielding the smoking firebrands like wands. The drawings suggested an ancient Tibetan practice of exorcism.[18] According to an old Tibetan text, the firebrands were used to vanquish evil spirits, or *sri*, often translated in English as "vampire."[19] It is believed that once a vampire took hold of a victim, it would slowly steal their vitality and eventually their life. In this cave the firebrands were set around the bodies to ward off the vampires; the stone barricade further protected the dead. And there they would lie undisturbed for over two thousand years.

Even though my life moved forward, something kept me connected to the people in the cave. Never did they feel gone. There was something beyond the bones, beyond the empty eye sockets, beyond the burial practices, the stories, the DNA, and beyond the artifacts. There was a much deeper connection, as though we shared on some level the same consciousness.

I imagined a world thousands of years from today when everything we know is forgotten and gone. What happens when *we* are the ones who are found? When those who come after search for answers—when they look deep into the quiet and still and glitter of the dark, what will they find? *Who* will they find?

Years passed. And then several more. The bone cave faded from my mind. Until one day I found myself in a deep dream-like meditation. I was back inside the cave. Except this time its crystal walls glittered brighter than ever. They glittered so brightly I didn't even need a light. And in the walls I saw the faces of those who came before. The faces carried a voice:

> Those who came before are not gone.
> They live in the shadows. In the light. In the
> sound. In the silence. Whispers of their existence
> are everywhere. In the richness of soil beneath
> our feet. In the air we breathe. In the beauty
> of the light that reflects everything it touches.
> They are a vast unseen mycelium, a living fabric
> born across time, enabling and guiding life
> for all that is.

We cannot understand it, and yet we know deep down it is the reason for our existence.

Listening to the message from the wall, I noticed a little girl in a corner of the cave. A girl from a time long before mine. She was watching me. Her hair was matted, her skin stained. She wore an old leathery dress-like covering, nearly the same colour as her skin. Her eyes were deep and dark—they spoke with confusion and curiosity. And hope. She didn't know why I was there or who I was. She was by herself. Alone. She didn't want me to leave her there. But I couldn't bring her with me. Could I? I extended a hand toward her. Her gaze shifted to the wall, and raising her thin, gentle arm, she pointed to a piece of it.

Then I came to.

I marched downstairs into my office. Opening a cabinet drawer, I reached my arm inside, brushing aside an array of papers and envelopes and knick-knacks. I found it: At the back of the cabinet was a handmade Nepali box, a treasure I'd hidden away years ago. I carefully pulled out the box and gently slid off its covering. The box was empty save for a single glittering piece of the coral-like cavern wall.

Those who came before are not gone.

A quote I'd once read by Carlo Levi flashed into my mind: "The future has an ancient Heart."[20]

Over billions of years of evolution, from the tallest mountains to Earth's great oceans, from the smallest ferns to the elder trees, the space in between, everything that has been and all that is now, there has arisen a great wisdom—a wisdom built into the very bones of our existence. An Earth wisdom. A Heart wisdom. One that transcends time and place and all conceptual limits. And through this wisdom all of nature is harmonized. As are we. It never deceives or lies to us. Just as our Heart never deceives or lies to us. And though we may not understand it, or see the shores to where we're going, if we let go enough, we can begin to soften into its guiding undercurrents. What is gravitating toward us? What is gravitationally moving away? What are our bodies telling us? What is our Heart telling us?

Where do we feel most at home? And what are we doing to nurture this feeling?

The more we choose to harmonize with the wisdom of our Heart, the more everything around us will harmonize with us. To walk this path is to honour it. Gradually, we will move forward through the bardos of life, healing ourselves, healing each other. We will build upon the bones of wisdom from those who came before, and bit by bit release the suffering of those who come after.

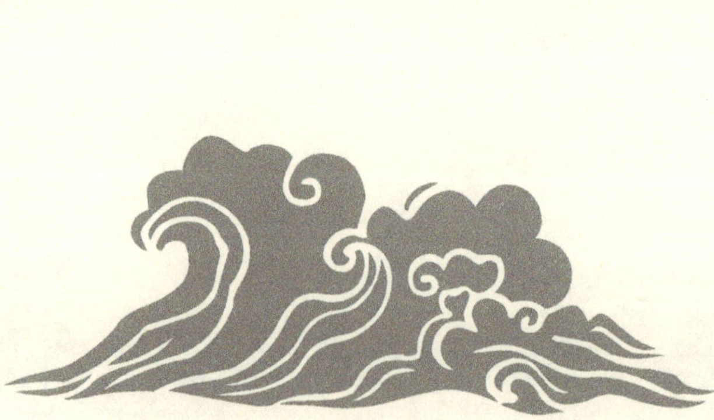

Shakyamuni

All experience is preceded by mind,
    Led by mind,
    Made by mind.
Speak or act with a peaceful mind,
    And happiness follows
Like a never-departing shadow.

—Gautama Buddha

GOLDEN FIELDS STRETCHED INTO the horizon under a cerulean sky. An old bodhi tree leaned eastward, its braided limbs reaching, decorated with a tangled web of colourful prayer flags.

Chantal and I gazed outward over the open meadow. Next to us were three sisters from a remote corner of the high Himalaya—Palma, Karma, and little Pemba, along with our Tibetan monk guide, Acharya Karma Sonam. We all stood in prayer position, in silence, our eyes closed and hands pressed firmly together at our hearts, uttering the words of Namo Buddhaya, Namo Dharmaya, and Namo Sanghaya—homage to the Buddha, homage to the practice (of the Dharma), and homage to those who hold our Heart.

Before us was a cluster of brick ruins, remnants of what was once the outer wall of a forgotten city. Some 2,500 years ago, young Siddhartha Gautama, prince of a small kingdom beneath the Himalayan foothills called the Shakyas, crossed the threshold of those gates for the last time, forever leaving his home, his family, his title, and his name. It was here that he began his quest of liberation from suffering, the start of a journey that would change everything.

The ruins, though sparse and weathered and long since abandoned, were far from bereft. An overwhelming feeling of reverence flowed through me in a moment that seemed as still as the lands before us—my mind moving neither forward nor back. Time seemed to fold into itself, closing the gap of centuries passed. I did not know what Prince Siddhartha was feeling when he travelled through those gates for the last time, but I did sense a great calmness—one that cast across the meadows by a gentle breeze. It was as if the wind carried a voice—the voice of suffering. All the suffering of the world. And as the wind spread over the fields, every bit of suffering became every bit of sound of the wind touching every blade of grass until it dissipated across the valley and returned to nothing.

I glanced at Acharya Karma. From behind his thick glasses his eyes were glowing and far-reaching as the fields. His maroon robes looked regal, his copper face burnished under the light of the Nepali sun. He gave me a smile and a nod. It was time to continue our pilgrimage.

The six of us returned to our miniature van, which looked more like a toaster, and with the searing heat often felt like being in one. One by one we squeezed ourselves into the tiny vehicle and, along with our driver, set off down the dusty dirt roads once again.

We'd only met Acharya Karma the day before. He was the head monk of the late Venerable Thrangu Rinpoche's monastery in Lumbini, in the southern lowlands of Nepal—mostly made famous because it is the birthplace of Gautama Buddha. The Thrangu monastery doubled as an abbey for some seventy nuns. At the time, however, all the nuns had left on a pilgrimage to Namo Buddha, Thrangu Rinpoche's primary monastery and former residence not far from Kathmandu. Fortunately for us, this left Acharya Karma alone at the monastery, and he was elated when we showed up at the entrance looking for a guide.

Unbeknownst to us until well into our journey, Acharya Karma took it to heart to meticulously prepare a day-long pilgrimage for us, one that would span from early dawn until well past sunset. We ventured all over the region visiting sites marked by significant events from Gautama Buddha's life, as well as from three of his preceding Buddhas: from Tilaurakot (the capital of the ancient Shakya Kingdom) to Gothawa, the birthplace of Krakuchhanda Buddha (the earliest of the three preceding Buddhas to Gautama), to Niglihawa, the birthplace of Kanakamuni Buddha (the second of the three preceding Buddhas), to the infamous Ashoka Pillar, where Emperor Ashoka marked the birthplace of Kanakamuni Buddha in 249 BC.

Speaking mostly Tibetan with the odd few words of English woven in, Acharya Karma passionately regaled us with stories, messages, and histories of the Buddhas. This was a bit puzzling for us at first since none of us knew there were preceding Buddhas to Gautama, most commonly known and referred to as *the* Buddha. Much of the time I could only make out at best half of what Acharya Karma was saying, which I felt a bit bad about. But I listened with steadfast determination nonetheless. I could tell there was wisdom in his words, and I didn't want to miss anything.

Chantal and the girls soaked in the surroundings as our little van pattered up and down ubiquitous dirt roads amid a sprawl of farmers' fields. As they come from the high mountains, where six-to-seven-thousand-metre peaks dominate the skyline in every direction, I wondered what thoughts were arising for Karma and Pemba and Palma about this very different part of their country—the sweltering heat, flat lowlands, and its darker-skinned inhabitants.

My thoughts often wandered back to the moment that brought us together—how a song, a dance, an embrace, could change the course of everything. Just a few years ago we hadn't known each other. Now we'd become like family. Some might call it fate. But I've come to realize it is the natural way of all things. When we are in harmony with ourselves, the world is in harmony with us. All any of us did was to have the courage to trust in the unspoken language of the Heart—to free ourselves of inhibition and open ourselves to each other and whatever may follow.

If the pyramid mountain had called me to its valley, it was a series of synchronistic events that had brought our paths together.

Shortly after my Sherpa companions and I retreated from the bone cave, Chantal and I and the rest of our team travelled westward to another small mountain village at over four thousand metres in elevation called Nar. It was here that we uncovered a karmic connection with a seven-year-old girl aptly named Karma. When we met Karma, she was teaching a group of children English numbers. It would turn out to be the most profound encounter of my life.

Karma and her little sister Pemba, who was only three years old at that time, had an unwavering thirst for education. Growing up in a harsh, semi-nomadic mountain village deep in the

Himalaya in a valley lost to the world for generations, and days away from any roads, electricity, toilets, health care, or schools, the girls and their family often had to defend their herds from snow leopards and risk life and limb venturing into even more extreme heights and terrain in search of *yarze gumpa* (a rare, fossilized caterpillar fungi the Chinese buy in droves). An outside education was not something readily available to them. Plus, that their family lived off less than two dollars per day created an even higher barrier for them than the mountains they resided among. Meeting with Karma's parents, Chantal and I discovered that education for their daughters was the biggest blessing they could ever hope for.

So we decided to work together, two pairs of parents coming together from different sides of the world, listening to each other, learning from each other, co-parenting to offer the best we could for two girls from one of the most remote and inaccessible places on Earth. It was the story I would recount in my book *A Story of Karma: Finding Love and Truth in the Lost Valley of the Himalaya.*

Over the years, the girls' parents, Sonam and Pema, and Chantal and I grew together as a family, forging a bond that spanned cultures, continents, time, and place. Together we managed to get Karma and Pemba placed in a safe boarding school in Kathmandu—one aligned with their unique Tibetan ethnic heritage—and eventually reunite them with their older sister Palma, who'd been recruited to a boarding school for orphans far away from her sisters and family.

We'd also embark on family trips together, often involving visits to different parts of Nepal. We'd witness how much their parents love their girls, and the care, equanimity, and selflessness they share with them.

We may not be biologically related, yet I know there is something much deeper at play—a connection spanning lifetimes. A connection embedded into our very lifeblood. It is a connection unperceived by the senses yet felt within the heart. And every day we choose each other, again and again. Not because we must, not for need or for want, but simply because of love.

We must "hold our children close to us," says Gabor Maté, for if we do not, "the ultimate cost is the loss of their ability to hold on to their own truest selves."[21] And although the girls and their parents are often apart and unable to see each other, or us, sometimes for years at a time, this has not diminished our feelings and the space we hold for each other. On the contrary, it has deepened the capacity, grace, and gratitude for the connection we share. Those kept in the Heart are always near.

In perhaps his most celebrated teachings, *The Dhammapada*, Gautama Buddha speaks of living a life from a place of love, acceptance, and compassion—a place in harmony with the Dharma and aligned with our truest Self, versus from a place where our truest Self is overshadowed by an afflicted mind. The one who lives from their truest Self "rejoices in this life. Rejoices in the next. Rejoices in both worlds." The one who does not "grieves in this life. Grieves in the next. Grieves in both worlds."[22]

Some interpret the words of Buddha "in this life," and "in the next" to mean *our* next life, or our reincarnated self. I also understand his words as referring to the ones who come after us—the children. When we instill love and compassion by honouring, softening into, and living the truest expression of who we are, so do we empower those who come after to do the same. When we do not, our afflictions are perpetuated into the next life—into "both worlds."

Never has this been clearer to me than when I am with the girls and witness the way they interact and shape the world around them. Pemba's teacher once shared an assignment he had his students write after the COVID lockdown, when Pemba and Karma's school in Kathmandu closed for several months and the girls returned to their village. In the words of a twelve-year-old Pemba:

> What I learned during lockdown:
>
> During lockdown I learned how much our parents love us, and how it is. I also learned to make meals and take care of our siblings. I learned to take care of our animals. And how life in the Himalayas is. They work really hard for food and shelter. Even though we say we are from the Himalayas, we didn't know how hard it is to survive in the Himalayas because we were in [boarding] school in very young years. It's because our parents don't want us to have a life like them.
>
> Love your parents.

Acharya Karma completed our pilgrimage at the Maya Devi Temple—Prince Siddhartha's birthplace. The sun had long since disappeared, now replaced with a vast and starry night sky blanketing the grounds in a dark stillness. Normally, the temple would have been teeming with crowds, thousands of people waiting in line, inching forward to catch a momentary glimpse of Buddha's birthplace. But now, since it was so late, there were few people about. All was quiet and at peace.

I don't know if it was because it was where Siddhartha was born, or whether it was because of the hundreds of thousands of people visiting the site each year with offerings of reverence and equanimity, or if it was because of the culmination of all the other places we had visited throughout the pilgrimage with Acharya Karma, or if it was because I was here with the ones I love, but there was a presence here I felt unlike any other, a deep presence that touched the very centre of my being.

The six of us began to do koras—a traditional Buddhist walking meditation—inside the temple around the modest brick foundation of the room in which Siddhartha had been born. After three rounds, we continued the koras outside, walking the brick path circling the temple. Around and around we paced, gently, calmly, unrushed, in silence, as though embracing the earth with each step and giving thanks to the air with each breath.

Karma, Pemba, and Palma walked hand in hand, taking comfort in each other's company. Acharya Karma strolled softly, his eyes reflecting the night sky. A piece of gold paint had broken free from a brick he'd placed his head against inside the temple and had now affixed to the centre of his forehead. "Touched by Buddha," he said with a youthful grin.

Chantal gazed into the open space with a look of gratitude, wonder, and calm. Later she would share with me, "Mike, this is an experience to remember—a special moment to be thankful for. To pay close attention to."

I felt something open inside myself. Through the stillness shone a new light. I had let go of all I was, of all I would be. Nothing remained other than a great peace within my heart.

On the grassy hillside south of the temple were dozens of pilgrims in deep prayer and meditation by candlelight, softly chanting a melodic chorus in a language I did not recognize.

Occasionally, we'd be stopped by others. "They want to take a photo with us," Acharya Karma would say, and we were happy to oblige.

"Why?" I asked afterwards.

"Because they see a great happiness in this family," he said, looking to us and the girls. "And they feel it is auspicious to share a moment with this happiness."

We continued our koras under the glitter of the night. I contemplated some of Acharya Karma's earlier words about Gautama Buddha, as I understood them. "We suffer because we grasp," he said. "We grasp because everything changes. So we must be with what is, and let go of all else. This is the path to truth and liberation."

Prince Siddhartha, once the prince of the Shakya, left behind everything he had and eventually returned to his people as Shakyamuni, Sage of the Shakya. He'd transcended the realm of suffering. By transcending Samsara, the endless cycle of death and rebirth, Prince Siddhartha had become a Buddha, a Tathagata, "one who comes and goes in accordance with the profoundest way of things"[23]—one who embodies the way of the Dharma.

It is believed the Dharma is at the very heart of Buddhism. And Buddhism is said to have arisen from the Dharma. Dharma is "that which is the basis of things, the underlying nature of things, the way things are; in short it is the truth about things, the truth about the world."[24]

Dharma is the formed, and it is the formless. It is the flowing river, and it is the burning fire. It is the wind, the air, and it is the earth. It is the unseen force that connects everything—from the most invisible particles to the grandest mountains. It harmonizes, balances, and enables all that is. It is memory and thought. It is consciousness. Not only of us, but all that is—from the animals to the trees to the soil and rocks. It is the singular truth of all that is and the most ancient of wisdoms. When we are in harmony with the Dharma, we are in harmony with the innate truth of all things. It is cross-dimensional, transcending time and space. All that was, all that is, all that will be is at once and at one with the Dharma, for it *is* the Dharma.

Buddha taught that the Dharma is also "the way we should act, for if we are to avoid bringing harm to both ourselves and others, we should strive to act not from illusion, but in a way that is true to the way things are, that accords with the underlying truth of things. Ultimately the only true way to act is in conformity with Dharma."[25]

In one of Buddha's teachings, he likened the Dharma to a man who had made a raft to cross a river, and who then let go of the raft once safely ashore. "As being like a raft," said Gautama Buddha, "I have taught you how Dharma is for the purpose of crossing over and not for the purpose of holding on to. Those who understand the similarity to a raft will let go even of the teachings and practices [Dharma], let alone what are not teachings and practices."[26]

The way of Dharma is not to be understood with the conceptual mind, for it is beyond concept. It is to be lived through practising loving kindness, compassion, equanimity, and joyful empathy, for this is the force that resides in emptiness and rests in stillness. It is the force that gives life to all that is and all that follows.

Days later, after bidding farewell to Acharya Karma, Karma, Pemba, and Palma, Chantal and I found ourselves at the Kathmandu airport, which was a stark contrast to the peaceful, serene, and still moments we had experienced together in Lumbini. The airport was packed with travellers. It smelled of smoke and sweat. Noise pervaded from every corner, including ear-piercing announcements over the loudspeakers fighting to be heard over the ceaseless clamour of the crowds. Throngs of people packed themselves in front of the few storefronts serving up cheap food and last-minute tourist trinkets.

Nevertheless, I still carried with me the feelings of Lumbini as though I was still there. Those moments had permeated into my very pores, into my very being, and I sat there in a hard plastic bucket chair simply present with all that had just happened, letting myself wander into nothingness.

An announcement blared over the loudspeakers. Our flight had been delayed by four hours. But it didn't matter. My heart and mind were at peace, and nothing in that moment could shake me from it.

And then something happened that I hadn't expected or experienced before.

I remember blinking, as I had done millions of times in my life before—nothing extraordinary about it. Except this time, when my eyes reopened after that millisecond of darkness, I now saw the world in a completely new way—all around me had become a vast spectrum of colours. I no longer saw the defined shapes of people and things but rather the energetic makeup of everything. It was as if I could see the interdependent particles coalescing as myriad brushstrokes flowing every which way, surrounding and travelling through everything, tracking every movement. I could still see people and objects, but they appeared as watermarks, faded behind auras and sinuous streams of colours. In every area we'd normally perceive as empty space were more coalescing colours, like rivers merging into each other from all directions. Some may wonder whether I was startled by this change in perception. But I was not. I remained still in the mindset of total presence and complete calmness.

I turned to Chantal, who for the last few hours had been suffering from a vicious migraine attack stemming from severe tension in her left shoulder. She is one of the most sensitive people I've ever known, empathetic to all energies, taking in the emotions of the people and places around her, and she'd been tormented by chronic pain episodes since she was a teenager. Lumbini had fully opened her up. And now the calamity of the Kathmandu airport—all its conflicting, intense, and overwhelming energies—was overloading her nervous system. She sat flopped over in her plastic bucket seat gently massaging her left shoulder. A look of distress and helplessness consumed her eyes and face.

I looked to her left shoulder, where I could see a mass of dark particles. Without moving a muscle, or letting Chantal know what it was I was experiencing or doing, I intuitively removed the particles from her neck and shoulder. I watched the whole black mass elevate from her body like a whirling cloud of tiny insects, and I gently sent the particles out the airport door and on to the tarmac, where they dissipated and disappeared. On another day, this act may have astonished me. But in that moment it was as natural as rinsing out a wound under the softness of water.

Chantal met my gaze. Life had returned to her eyes.

"How are you feeling?" I asked.

"The pain has stabilized." A faint smile had returned to her lips.

Still I did not share with her what was happening. It didn't help that I didn't actually *know* what was happening. And even if I did, I had no idea how to explain it.

Eventually, my vision faded, returning to its previous state. Colours disappeared or dulled. Empty space became empty space once again. And I could no longer perceive the makeup of the energetic forces around me.

And that was okay. For anything else would be to grasp. To hold. To cling.

> *Those who understand the similarity to a raft will let go even of the teachings and practices.*

Words of René Daumal surfaced in my mind: "What is above knows what is below, what is below does not know what is above... There is an art to finding your way in the lower regions by the memory of what you have seen when you were higher up. When you can no longer see, you can at least still know."[27]

So I take comfort in what has come and what has gone. Letting go of the raft that is no longer needed. Knowing that behind the muddied water of our afflicted minds there is a natural, beautiful, harmonizing, and eternal land fluent within itself. And I choose to rest within that.

Brent

What is your dream?
Not the one you're thinking about.
But the one you feel deep inside

When all else is calm, quiet, and still.

THE WHOLE VALLEY WAS STILL. A great calmness permeated the rocks and mountains, and the streams and tarns. Not even a breath of wind could be felt.

Chantal and I were making our way up Mount Matier, the highest peak in the Joffre Group, a glaciated and rugged subset range of Canada's Coast Mountains. We moved lightly over the rocky terrain. It was an area familiar to us, except this time the landscape was markedly different. Three years prior, a large part of Mount Matier's neighbouring peak, Mount Joffre, caved off, releasing an enormous avalanche of boulders, many the size of cars or houses, which came crashing through the valley with such force it tore through the trees for miles, clearing them aside like matchsticks. The whole scene looked like some sort of post-apocalyptic aftermath—greyed, dusted, destroyed. And yet the valley was at peace.

We quietly scampered across the vast swath of broken granite, over twisted old-growth and uprooted stumps, and scrambled over countless mounds of mangled rock and earth. We skirted silt-laden banks around pools of glacial runoff—remnants of the valley creek—and boulder-hopped newly cut streams carrying the scents and colourful ribbons of liquefied minerals from the broken mountain.

Not long up the debris field, however, we were stopped in our tracks. For above us appeared a great bull moose, postured as still as the mountain of rock beneath him. He was calm, gentle, at peace. We looked at each other in silence, like tiny fragments affixed in time and into the scene at large.

And in that moment I somehow sensed a feeling of completeness—completeness within myself, completeness with Chantal, and completeness with the natural surroundings. Chantal and I stood motionless, as though we were witnessing something sacred—understanding without understanding. In time the moose turned to the treeline, faded into the forest, and was gone.

"Is it just me or did that moose's presence feel like Brent?" Chantal wondered aloud. But there was nothing more to speak about. The moose's presence did feel like our dear friend Brent. The entire day seemed to be absorbed by his presence. And we knew without a doubt that if Brent had not been climbing Mount Manaslu in the Himalaya, he would have been here with us.

Every now and then we meet someone who truly sees us. Not with their eyes but with their heart. And our hearts respond.

For me, that was Brent.

Brent moved through life with open kindness. There was a gentleness about him and unfettered joy in his spirit. And he was deeply, deeply sensitive to the world.

In the fifteen years I knew him, not once did he speak ill of anyone. He'd often go out of his way to help others in need—friends and strangers alike—especially when no one else was watching—even though he was struggling with his own mental health and had been diagnosed with schizophrenia. Brent was my best friend, and he was my little brother in the mountains. I trusted him with my life.

Although we shared countless adventures in the mountains together—some of my very best—it felt like our time together had been cut short. Three days after Chantal and I stood together with that moose, I received a call from Brent's father. "Brent died," were the words that came through from the other end of the line. Those two words have forever burned themselves into my mind. At first, they seemed incomprehensible, as though my mind refused to accept them. Surely, this was a grand mistake, that something had been lost in translation and we'd all see him again very soon. But the reality was true. Brent had died in the Himalaya near the summit of Mount Manaslu.

There's a great clarity that occurs when a loved one dies. A sudden sharpness of memory and thought, at least for a time. It's as if all the seemingly unimportant moments—the random mannerisms, things that were said, certain looks, the way someone laughed or moved—all come to life. I've found some of these memories slowly begin to fade over time, and yet some remain as vivid as the moment they happened—just like the day Brent and I met.

I was hosting a leadership workshop at Simon Fraser University, in Vancouver, where Brent was a student. At the first break, Brent approached me.

"Mike, what advice would you have to become a public speaker?"

"Well, you speak…in public," I responded lightheartedly.

"But I've been diagnosed with schizophrenia."

I'm not sure what came over me. At the time I'd never met anyone with schizophrenia, or any severe mental illness for that matter. But all I responded with was a simple "So?"

It was the spark that would create a lifelong friendship for us both in and out of the mountains.

At that time Brent had never climbed a mountain, but he was intrigued by them. In fact, the one clarifying thought he'd had shortly after his release from the psychiatric ward, which I learned years later, was to be the first person diagnosed with schizophrenia to climb Mount Everest—and not only for himself.

"I remember what it feels like to be blindsided by an illness that just hits you out of the blue," Brent once said. "I never saw it coming. I remember that feeling of being terrified. Of being stuck. And of being hopeless."

At the time of his diagnosis, he couldn't drive a car or read the newspaper or attend classes or hang out with his closest friends, but Chomolungma (as the Tibetans call it) gave him strength. It gave him hope. And he wanted to do what he could to give that hope to others. It was a call to action.

With the full support of his family, Brent dedicated the next fifteen years of his life to helping those with mental illnesses—especially youth—as well as reshaping the narrative of mental health at a time when it was still severely stigmatized and misunderstood. He finished his degree, graduating as the valedictorian of his class. And he became an accomplished speaker, impacting the lives of thousands.

Amid all his triumphs, however, he never gave up on his dream to climb Mount Everest. It was something I always admired in him.

"[Mount Everest] just calls to me," he said. "To pursue and fulfill a dream, or at least pursue it with everything you've got I think is something important for us to do as humans if we have the opportunity. I spent many days in bed, not being able to do anything, in the psych ward. To have an opportunity to do something like this is rare. You've got to make the most of those opportunities."

Brent began taking all the right steps. They were small steps, at first—learning how to hike smaller mountains and taking basic mountaineering courses, and then climbing larger and larger mountains. Before long Brent had climbed Aconcagua and Denali, the highest mountains in South America and North America. He'd climbed Lobuche in the shadow of Everest, and countless peaks in the coastal mountain ranges and around his hometown of Vancouver. In the fall of 2021, he'd embarked to climb Mount Manaslu, the eighth-highest mountain in the world, as a preparation climb for Mount Everest the following spring.

When Brent and I first started climbing together, I was a little apprehensive. After all, I knew very little about schizophrenia, only what I'd heard about in various news stories. And being in the mountains is about trusting the ones you're with. But the more we journeyed into the mountains together, the more I realized Brent was one of the most solid people I knew. There was something about him—something incredibly in tune with the rhythm of the natural world—the nuances, the clarity, the calmness, the wisdom. He moved through the wilderness as though he was part of it: Measured. Balanced. Respectful. Watchful. At ease. And he always put his friends ahead of the summit. "Brent, you're the sanest person I know," I once told him.

For more than a decade we climbed peaks throughout the BC coastal ranges and northern Cascades. We trained together two to three times a week. Sometimes we'd carry heavy packs up steep trails. Sometimes we'd rock climb. Sometimes we'd run trails up and down the hills in our backyard. And despite the often seriousness of our endeavours, we'd never lose our lightheartedness. We'd laugh for what seemed like hours about things neither of us remembered. We were as content to bask in joyful banter as we were to delve into the deep conversations of life or the wide spaces of silence.

But throughout all the years Brent and I climbed together, one of the most memorable times for me wasn't on some epic mountain or adventure. It was a little winter half-day hike in the outskirts of my hometown of Squamish to a warming shelter called the Red Heather Hut. It was a characteristic west coast winter day. Cloud-veiled and moody, with unending drizzle in the valley. But it didn't deter us—we knew what lay before us.

When we arrived at the trailhead, it was covered with a foot of snow, and the rain had turned to soft white flakes. That day I donned my skis, and Brent his snowshoes (which was ironic as Brent was a much better skier than me), and together we began to trudge up the never-ending switchbacks. The sound of silence only broken by the crunch of snow underfoot and the rhythm of my skins whizzing along the icy crust. Back and forth, and back and forth, and back and forth the switchbacks we climbed beneath towering, snow-dusted, subalpine old growth.

In time we reached the warming hut. After a snack and a drink, and without tarrying too long, we were ready to make our way back. As we set out, I began to ski ahead. My skis enabled me to cruise down one switchback and wait for Brent to catch up. I'd then ski down the next, again waiting for Brent. *There must be a better way to do this*, I thought to myself.

In all the times Brent and I had been out, not once had he brought a crazy carpet with him—except for that day.

We have a crazy carpet. "Do we have any rope?" I asked Brent. Sure enough, for some reason unknown to me, Brent had brought a short rope. We tied one end around his waist, and the other around mine. Brent propped himself on his crazy carpet, and I pointed my skis downhill, and off we went.

With the icy crust, we picked up speed almost immediately and soon began soaring down the switchbacks. Some of the banked corners we took with such velocity that Brent nearly launched into the forest until the rope caught him at the last moment, whipping him down the next turn. The two of us were howling with laughter as we flew down the trail. Some of the other hikers coming up would have heard us before seeing us, with just enough time to move aside as we rocketed by them.

I realized many years later that it was never about climbing mountains. It was just about being out there with my friend.

A few days after Brent's death, his mother shared a story with me.

When Brent was released from the psychiatric ward, his mother brought him to their home. For Brent, it was too terrifying or traumatizing to leave the house. For the first two days, he and his mother would simply sit on their sofa, sometimes talking, sometimes just sitting in silence. On the third day his mother said to Brent, "We're not doing this anymore." And she took Brent out on a little nature hike near their home. While Brent had pursued athletics throughout his teenage years, he'd never really spent much time simply walking or hiking in nature. Brent gazed up at the soaring treetops. "This is where I need to be," was all he said.

A dear friend and clinical counsellor once said to me, "The separation between humans and nature is the trauma from which all others follow."

It reminded me of what my friend Curtis, a member of the Tahltan First Nation and former Chairman of the Tahltan Central Council, had shared with me about the importance of his people's ancient practice of youth journeying out onto the land by themselves. How these trips into nature allow the youth to develop the mental tools they inevitably need later in life—tools not only for their own benefit but for their community as well. And how, through the loss of this practice, he has observed youth lose connection with their traditional and ancestral wisdom, and the power of the visions they would receive as a result.

Recent studies among other First Nations communities show how strong ties to the land and land-based forms of learning and healing directly impact not only a youth's well-being and mental health but also the degree to which they are received by their communities and see themselves as valuable contributors to one another.[28]

Indigenous Peoples' understanding of mental health goes far beyond noting the connection to the land. In his research on schizophrenia and shamanism in traditional cultures, psychiatrist

Julian Silverman observed how many Indigenous cultures accept and embrace psychosis as a form of "expanded consciousness."[29] This perception runs counter to "modern culture" that regards psychosis as an illness to be corrected, perpetuating and intensifying the accompanying anxieties.

According to academic and writer the late Joseph Campbell, psychosis can be viewed as "an effort to recover and restore a lost balance," to better understand, garner insight, and shape the environment and world in which we live. "In order to be helpful, however, the doctor has to understand the imagery of mythology. He has to understand what these signs and signals are that this person totally out of contact with the rationally oriented individual is trying to bring forth."[30]

Perhaps what was deemed psychosis was not an illness at all but a much deeper symptom of a sound mind and spirit trying to cope in an unsound environment, with the simultaneous repression of what is natural, unseen, and innately harmonious.

"What if those with mental illness simply have unique abilities?" Brent once mused. "To empathize more. To see the world more clearly. To have enhanced creativity to find and create solutions. What if we harnessed those powers?"

What if Brent was right, and psychosis offered critical clues to our continued evolution—clues to align ourselves with the sacred wisdom of Earth? Guiding us like Tibetan chortens in the mountains—ancient structures designed to embody and spread the wisdom of the Buddha—so we may continue to sustain and be in service to the creation of life.

I often think about Brent's last moments. What they must have been like, high up on the mountain. According to his companion, Tendi Sherpa, they were approaching eight thousand metres above sea level just as the sun cast its first rays over all the Himalaya. The skies were clear. Brent sat down for a drink and a bite, and breathed his last breaths, taking it all in. He was smiling when he passed.

Curtis once told me his grandmother could tell when a spirit had left the body, sometimes days before the body died. I believe a part of Brent was there with Chantal and me in that moose. But in my heart I know it was never a farewell. For I know Brent is out there, in another form, perhaps one better suited to do his work. I hear the clarity of his words, words he shared with me not long after his death: "The path is straight. Do not deviate."

Each of us has a path, a natural way. The path may curve and bend, but it is also straight. Sometimes we try to intervene. To overthink. To overmanage. To repress. To suppress. To deviate. To expect. To see. When what we can do to create harmony, grace, and peace in the world is to have the courage to listen, to live simply, and simply live the full expression of our truest self and in harmony with our deepest Truth. In harmony with the innate sacred wisdom of Earth.

"The aim is not to *see*," says Joseph Campbell, "but to realize that one *is*, that essence; then one is free to wander as that essence in the world. Furthermore: the world too is of that essence. The essence of oneself and the essence of the world: these two are one...There is no separateness. Thus, just as the way of social participation may lead in the end to a realization of the All in the individual, so that of exile brings the hero to the Self in all."[31]

Brent lived his truth until the end, moving with confidence and grace through the final bardo of his life, at last liberating himself from limitation and suffering. And like the words of a book that exist in the unseen space beyond ink and page, I continue to feel Brent's presence. Ever he is there in the vast expanse of the verdant forests. Where the light of the sun meets the white cloud. In the silence of the great stony mountains.

Stillness

(written shortly after Brent's passing)

Stillness.
It is the beginning.
And the end
of all things.

Like the pool of water,
returned to its natural state.
Or the tiny droplet,
taking rest on a delicate leaf.

It is the eye of the deer,
a dark and endless orb
as deep as the universe,
filled with a billion stars.

It is the great owl,
extending from branch and root.
Seeing from behind yellow eyes.
Hearing what cannot be heard.

Heavenly clouds basking
before the golden sun.
The great snowy mountain
still as stone.
Rays of morning light
dipping through treetops.

It speaks the language of the earth,
a language shaped and carved and created
over a hundred million years.

It is the language of the Heart.
It is where we come alive.
It is what we call Home.

And so, as long as I draw breath,
I do my best to move toward that stillness.
To be that stillness.
For that is where I find myself.
It is where we find each other again.

Golden

Gold gathers in silence.

No more words.
Rising sun, you release us
From the guards, the thieves,
The nights within us and without.

—Rumi

THE WALL OF WHITE MOUNTAINS GREW larger as our tiny fixed-wing Otter droned over the frosted Alaskan woodland.

"I moved here for the commute," cracked the voice through my headset. I glanced at our pilot, whose bristled face and black shades were overshadowed by a sun-eating grin.

Behind me in the snug cabin Klemen gave a thumbs-up. Beside him was a heap of our mountaineering gear strapped under a mesh net. Klem's weather-hardened Slovenian disposition had metamorphosed into one of youthful delight. I'm sure my face mirrored his.

I remembered Brent's words after he'd returned from Denali: "Go to Alaska. It'll be fun." The Alaskan mountains had opened something in him—some vast and awestruck place where wonder and curiosity had no bounds. Now I heard his silence, and little thirteen-year-old Pemba's words: "Be safe out there, Mikari." Mikari was a nickname she'd given me. "And be kind to your body."

Occasionally, a blast of arctic wind struck our hollow aircraft, rattling me from my child-like stupor and reminding me of what we were heading into. But one look to the serrated horizon and I was again overcome with mountain fever.

Mount Denali and Mount Foraker rose from a sea of formidable black and white pinnacles. Before them the great Ruth Glacier opened as though the mountains themselves had parted, creating a two-kilometre-wide, 960-metre-deep frozen wonder. This remnant of the last ice age sinewed the toothed landscape like an enormous serpent.

Soon we were no longer eyeing the peaks from afar, and our plane was an insignificant red dot against a canvas of whites and greys and blacks. Waves of vertical rock hugged our aerial path. They were like ice-laden castles—stark, terrifying, magnificent.

Our pilot threaded around one of the stone columns, tipping a wing toward the earth and pulling our gaze into the yawning crevasses. His face seemed etched with the same lines in the granite beside us. He knew these mountain passages like his neighbourhood roads...or at least that's what I told myself.

"The Root Canal is just ahead of us," broke through my headset. The Root Canal is a keyhole gap that opens into a small stadium-like glacier called the Root Canal Glacier. Otherwise concealed by towering peaks, the Root Canal Glacier sits perched above the Great Gorge, the deepest part of the Ruth Glacier. This gorge is nearly 2,743 metres deep, deeper than even the Grand Canyon.

Our aircraft began its descent. Between the imposing walls of rock and crumbling ice I could see a snow-covered plateau just big enough for a near-impossible horseshoe-shaped landing strip.

Following a surprisingly soft touchdown, Klem and I hopped from the aircraft, its engine still running. We unloaded our bags of gear as swiftly as we could. Standing in the fresh thigh-high powder, we gave a thumbs-up to the pilot and watched our way home take flight. Before the white flurry could settle, the aircraft had vanished.

We'd been thrust into stillness—out of the world we knew and into one of cold stone and snow and ice. The peaks nurtured huge hanging seracs—masterworks sculpted over hundreds of thousands of years suspended in perfect equilibrium.

Mount Denali loomed high on the distant horizon.

Thoughts from Peter Matthiessen's *The Snow Leopard* surfaced: "The secret of the mountains is that the mountains simply exist, as I do myself: the mountains exist simply, which I do not."[32]

Or as Jane Austen asked, "What are [we] to rocks and mountains?"[33]

We set, fortified, and tied down our tent with drawstrings and buried anchors, and dug out a makeshift kitchen. Then Klem and I turned our gaze back to the Moose's Tooth and our objective for the next day: the infamous Ham and Eggs Couloir, a 914-metre vertical passage of ice and snow.

First climbed in 1975 by Thomas Davies, John Krakauer, and Nate Zinsser in a thirty-three-hour push, the route got its name when Zinsser stated, "If we had some ham, we could have some ham and eggs, if we had some eggs."[34]

Klem opened *Deep Survival* by Laurence Gonzales, reading aloud in his thick Slovenian accent: "'The earth moved' can have different meanings in different circumstances. [Fear] can make you feel more alive, because it is an integral part of saving your own life."[35] Closing the book, he turned his chapped face back to the mountain. "But are we running because we're afraid? Or are we afraid because we're running?"[36]

It was a good question. *What am I seeking? What am I chasing? What do I fear?*

Somehow, losing over twenty friends in the mountains had softened him.

My mind desperately tried to find a new rhythm to match what stood before us. The Moose's Tooth jutted from the glacier like a fang, its enormous walls so sheer not even snow could stick to them. Everything about this place should have told me to leave. But running begets fear, and fear begets suffering.

I thought back to the words of Trungpa Rinpoche: "When we are afraid of waking up and afraid of experiencing our own fear," he said, "we create a cocoon to shield ourselves. We may think that we have quieted our fear, but we are actually making ourselves numb with fear. We are so afraid of our own fear that we deaden our hearts...When we are constantly recreating our basic patterns of behaviour and thought, we never have to leap into fresh air or onto fresh ground."[37]

Suddenly, an undetected shift released a mammoth-sized chunk of ice from a nearby serac, tearing the silence with an explosion of thunder and rumbling. Klem and I watched the white landslide sweep down the mountain and settle in a cloud of snow.

If we can create our own cocoon, can we not choose to dissolve it? Bit by bit, can we begin to seep into its cracks and expose our own dark corners? Would this not be the purpose of life? To warm to our deepest fear so it supports us like a faithful friend. To edge into our discomfort just as we would ease onto sharp stones beneath bare feet. After all, "the miracle," as

Thich Nhat Hanh said, "is not to walk on thin air or water, but to walk on Earth."[38]

What is life but a practice to walk on the earth? A practice to "exist simply." A practice to take refuge in the presence of what is.

Despite the intimidating mountain faces, there was clarity in the open skies—a voiceless call to go to the mountain. I could not help but feel Brent had something to do with it. We prepared to set out early the next morning.

The full moon rose, and we rose with it. Our head torches pulsed like pale stars in the darkness. The scent of the icy Alaskan air flooded my body with each breath, and the crust of the snow creaked beneath each step. Distant galaxies glowed overhead, and all around us mountains slept.

Not long after setting out from camp our direction abruptly shifted. Horizontal became vertical, and we swiftly adapted. The fronts of our steel crampons bit into the hardened snow. The tips of our tools clawed into the ice. Skyward we moved, methodically, carefully, purposefully.

Klem manoeuvred up the mountain with precision and vigour, clearing a trail through half a metre of fresh snow that somehow stuck to the funnel of ice. Growing up at the foot of the Julian Alps, he'd had the perfect training grounds. In his younger years he'd ventured to some of the most challenging mountains—from climbing the infamous Trango Tower and completing the first ascent of its neighbour, Trango Monk, in Northern Pakistan's Karakoram, to putting up new routes in Patagonia's Fitz Roy range. He is the strongest climber I know, but he almost never talks about his feats. "When you are out there, somewhere in no man's land…there are no gold medals. No heroes," he says. "We are all the same vulnerable little laughing people of Earth."

We continued up the frozen path, hollowed between the imposing walls of rock. The higher we climbed, the more persistent the streams of spindrift became. Each new stream felt more intense than the last, pummelling us like an unrelenting firehose. All I could do was cling to the ice, even though the muscles in my arms felt as though they were about to burst.

"At what point is this an avalanche?" I grunted, enduring the ice flow from under the hood of my Gore-Tex jacket, cursing even though I knew no one could hear me.

Words a Tahltan Elder once shared with me rang in my ears: "You must have respect for the mountain, for the mountain has no respect for you."

More grunting. More cursing.

The current would lapse for a moment. *Go. Go now!* All waking thought returned to the next few moves.

Hours turned. Our crampons and ice tools left the walls chipped and scarred. Calves began to burn, yearning to stand on something flat. Face and fingers grew numb and senseless. Ice-chalked gloves froze into grotesque figures. Arms felt like lead, and each move was another arduous undertaking.

Why am I here? I don't belong here. Give up now. Go home. But some rooted stubbornness shut it all down, and we kept moving in only one direction. I knew the pain would end. It must. And it did.

The couloir widened and the mountain's passage started to ease, revealing a windswept summit ridge. I checked my watch:

8:30 p.m. The sun rested heavy over the skyline, casting its evening rays upon the crystallized granite.

And then the light struck the mountain in precisely the right way. Millions of flecks of gold gilded in the rock awoke in a spectacular display of ethereal glitter. The stone-faced mountain, which had been draped in shades of black and grey, had transformed into a shimmering pinnacle. I was awestruck. An overwhelming sense of gratitude streamed through me, rekindling my cold limbs and tired mind. Never in my life had I been embraced by such a divine gift of the mountain.

May we never forget how to leap into fresh air or onto fresh ground.

I caught up to Klem, and for a moment we sat in the snow, alone from the world. We watched the glowing range of giants under violet skies as waves of spindrift danced spirals around us. I tried sipping water from my canteen, but ice touched my lips. It was time for us to descend.

One by one we rappelled down the mountain. What took so much effort and toil to climb we slid by with ease.

Twenty-two hours after setting out, with countless rappels and three pairs of frozen gloves each, we were back at our camp.

"How we abuse our feet," Klem ruminated with a dry smile, pulling off his frozen boots.

After nourishing ourselves with some noodle soup and sharing a frozen apple, we burrowed into our sleeping bags. Though our bodies were spent, our minds were awake over what we'd just done. It was one of the most challenging climbs of my life. But climbing such a peak in this incredible mountain wilderness, and with the cloudless skies on our backs, had exceeded my wildest dreams. *Thank you, Brent.*

Somewhere outside our tent I heard a man and a woman in animated conversation. It sounded like they were speaking English, though the voices were muffled and I couldn't make out the words. They sounded full of life. Content.

"Do you hear that? Did another party arrive during our climb?" I wondered aloud.

Klem heard them too. "Yes, who is that?" But neither of us had the energy to step outside to investigate.

When we awoke a few hours later, there was no one there. No new footsteps. Unbroken snow. Klem and I looked at each other. On some other level the voices made sense. *Why wouldn't memory linger in such places?*

I turned to the mountain, tracing our route with new eyes. The passage we'd climbed was no longer foreign, no longer separate, no longer something to be feared but only respected. Every swing. Every step. Every kick. Every curse. Every move. Every emotion and every piece of the route. Somewhere between the mountain and me something new had been created, and something else had ceased to be.

"The mountains have no meaning," said Matthiessen. "They *are* meaning; the mountains *are*."[39]

To the west, crystal skies shone over the entire Alaskan range, and my face soaked in the warmth of the morning sun. I felt my mind melting into the distance. No longer running. Nowhere left to go. Hope and fear dissolved into the horizon like streams of white cloud, liberated.

Perhaps here, where the earth dances with the sky, we truly exist. Beyond origin and destination, where all directions merge and all that ever is and was becomes and reflects into itself. Ever present yet never grasped. Always changing and always complete. Empty yet infinite. Nowhere and everywhere.

And perhaps it is here our memories also reside, etched into the fabric of all existence, passing beyond the limits of the psyche and shadow of stone. Golden imprints to the light.

The gift of Earth is not something to be grasped, nor something to be captured or kept in secret or in dark places. Like the sunrise, it is something to be observed, to feel. When we truly behold Earth, we begin to hear its language, and we find we are already home. We realize what we've been seeking is what we've been running from: the sacred and vulnerable place from which springs our innate nature. When we allow ourselves to truly rest in the hearth of Earth—the unabated stillness of the peaks and valleys, the ever-flowing rivers and far-reaching forests—only then will we come face to face with ourselves once again. We will feel the earth move, and ourselves—and it won't be terrifying but beautiful. We will finally cease to run, and so too cease to fear.

Returning to the village of Talkeetna was like waking from a dream. Sunburnt and numbed from the cold, I re-entered the ranger station to let the rangers know we were back from our climb and to inform them of the mountain's conditions. No doubt I had the same look of hundreds of others who'd come back from the mountains.

A veteran ranger greeted me.

"Y'all have a good time?"

Adrenalin still pulsed through me. I regaled her (and inadvertently all the other tourists) with our climb of the Moose's Tooth.

Just as I was turning to leave, something compelled me to go on.

"There was something else," I began, glancing to all those whose eyes were still on me. "This may sound strange. The night we returned, as we lay in our tent, we heard a conversation between a man and a woman. We didn't think much of it—until we awoke the next morning only to find no one had arrived. No new tracks in the snow."

All fell quiet.

"That doesn't sound strange at all," said the seasoned ranger, her eyes piercing mine. "Some who went into those mountains did not come back."

Kūkai

A full moon hangs in the sky.
Moonlight reflects on thousands of rivers
and on all the jars of water.
The Buddha-mind is calm in the Great Void.
It dwells in all people in the world of illusion.
A water moon in a round mirror is deceptive.
So is the self we put on.

—Kūkai

I'D BEEN DRAWN TO VISIT JAPAN ever since I was a teenager. Something about Zen Buddhism captivated me. There is something so incredibly simple, yet infinitely enigmatic, about its teachings and koans—the seemingly paradoxical anecdotes meant to provoke a transcendence of logical reasoning. Like the autostereogram pictures that first appear as a maze of two-dimensional colours but then reveal an underlying three-dimensional image hidden within, it was as if the koans presented the answers we seek both right in front of us and at the same time veiled in riddle. As with the autostereograms, it seemed the way into the koan was to stop trying to see what is "hidden."

When I was younger, I didn't have the money to go. And later in life most of my trips to Asia with Chantal were focused on Nepal to be with Karma and Pemba and their family. Chantal and I were there for Karma's first day of school, but ten years later, as we headed back to see her graduate from high school, we decided we'd take the opportunity to visit Japan. The small oceanside village of Kamakura would be the start of our pilgrimage.

Several kilometres inland atop a small mountain behind the charming village sits a bronze Buddha once housed in a temple. In the fifteenth century a great tsunami ravaged the area. So violent was its force it reached all the way to the top of the mountain, sweeping all the buildings and the temple away. The Buddha of Kamakura, however, was left unscathed and has sat under the open skies ever since.

Chantal and I stood beneath a crooked Japanese pine tree, which marked the gates of Hasedera, a 1,300-year-old Japanese temple. Being at Hasedera was like wandering through a fairy tale: the meticulously pruned trees and thick blankets of matcha moss, the white sand corridors lining the pathways, and the luminous koi with their feathered tails tracing shapes in the water.

"Consider yourself lightly; consider the world deeply," wrote Miyamoto Musashi in his final short work, *Dokkōdō* (*The Way of Walking Alone*)[40] one week before he died. I wondered if the way the Japanese practised being with nature was a means to honour this perspective.

As we strolled the temple grounds, we came upon a structure housing a giant wooden *rinzo*—a rotating bookshelf containing thousands of Buddhist scriptures. Inlaid in the walls were several smaller bronze Tibetan prayer wheels. Curiously, these were the only Tibetan prayer wheels we saw in Japan. (I later discovered one of the monks had suggested the bronze Tibetan wheels as the large wooden one was getting too worn to spin every day.)

"How would you say Tibetan Buddhism differs from that of Zen?" Chantal mused.

"I suppose if Tibetan Buddhism is like the clapping of thunder, abrupt and direct, Zen is like the gentle flowing stream through a tranquil forest."

Amid the intricate temples and shrines and lush pathways, we came before a nondescript cave that disappeared into the mountainside, its entrance marked by a single red *torri*—a traditional Japanese gate used to demarcate the transition from the ordinary world into the sacred.

I felt myself drawn in.

The cavern was dank and dark, save for the faint orange glow of flickering candles. It smelled of earth and wet rock, and its walls seeped and dripped. Statues of Buddhist deities and monks of old peered out from sunken shadows. All was deeply quiet.

Chantal and I took our time pacing the cave's narrow corridors, remaining in silent meditation.

When we finally re-emerged into daylight, Chantal turned to me as though a new energy had soaked into her pores. "There's a high spiritual presence in there," she remarked. "And strong masculine energy—as if someone spent a lot of time meditating there, facing the wall."

I'd felt it too. Something very old resided within this mountain.

Before we left, I pulled an *omikuji* (fortune paper) from a box. "How do you go across a dangerous steep ridge at ease?" The question gave me pause, not only because it had me thinking about steep mountain ridges.

Hasedera had created a small opening for our journey. An opening to what, I did not know. But it was time to leave the sanctity of this temple. From here Chantal and I would continue our pilgrimage westward to Fuji-san (Mount Fuji), Japan's beloved "immortal" mountain.

Chantal and I made our way up pumiced paths beneath wind-bent hemlock and hinoki cypress. Gradually, the trees dispersed, giving way to crumbled slopes of black volcanic rock dotted with strange green plants and an endless horizon.

Fuji-san has long been a source of inspiration and meditation and is deeply rooted in Japan's cultural identity and history.

Rising from open seas and forested hillsides, surrounded by flowering cherry blossoms and placid lakes, the symmetrical cone-shaped volcano unfolds into the sky like an enormous fan. Stark yet soft. Strong yet humble.

Following a warm and nourishing stay at one of the mountain "stations"—a modest lodging usually run by a Japanese family—Chantal and I awoke around 2 a.m. to begin our hike to the summit. The higher we climbed, the more enshrouded we were by cloud. At times I could barely make out the path before us, my head torch unable to pierce through the dense fog.

We plodded along at a steady pace until our path joined the infamous Yoshida trail about two hundred metres below the summit. Rounding a bend, I nearly stepped backwards in disbelief. Before me was an unbroken string of headlamps—hundreds of people, Japanese and tourists alike, all in a queue to reach the summit. Chantal and I waited to file in.

Eventually, the line began inching forward. Two or three paces. Stop. Repeat. Feelings of frustration and impatience arose within me as thick clouds released an unremitting torrent of rain. Winds at fifty to sixty kilometres per hour complemented my mood. With each new gust the entire line halted to a complete standstill. *We can't keep stopping every time there is a gust of wind!* I thought as I lightly hopped in place to stay warm. The path was too narrow and clogged to move forward or backward, and with every passing minute I felt the cold wetness soaking through my outer layers.

Something from Hasedera lingered in my mind: *Be at ease. Be at ease. Be at ease. Breathe.*

No outward view. Nothing to see...But there is inward view.

Why did I get the feeling the mountain was one giant koan, taunting me?

I remembered the words I once read from legendary alpinist Walter Bonatti: "I don't deny that there can be an element of escapism in mountaineering, but this should never overshadow its real essence, which is not escape but victory over your own human frailty."[41]

Is life not like the mountain? Is life not but one great meditation? A practice to realize and move through our own frailty?

It was the longest two hundred vertical metres I've ever spent on a mountain.

Chantal and I reached the top of Fuji-san at sunrise, though no sunrise could be seen. Cold and wet and drenched to the skin, we embraced each other for a moment, and after a warming cup of miso soup, we began our descent. Nothing to achieve.

Winds and rain storming
The mountain always changing
The red sun rises.

I'd learned of a small temple on the outskirts of Kyoto from a dear friend and Buddhist scholar, Paula Arai. In her book *Painting Enlightenment*, Paula speaks of a sacred place where a thousand forgotten gravestones from centuries past had been collected and brought together in unity around a central stone stupa. The place is called Adashino Nembutsu Temple.

"Birth and death show us the nature of emptiness," Paula writes. "When viewed nearby, it looks as though there is birth and death. However, when viewed from the plentitude of our boundlessness, there is no birth and death...In a fundamental way, death unleashes our capacity to nourish each other."[42]

When Chantal and I arrived at the Adashino temple we found the grounds largely empty, which was a refreshing respite from the bustling and tourist-packed streets of Kyoto.

The collection of one thousand forgotten gravestones stands in the centre of the grounds. A shallow rock partition surrounds the stones, and a single gate serves as its entrance. Walking through the gate, I felt a marked shift in energy. Some of the gravestones were so old they were partially buried with moss. Others were so weatherworn they'd lost all their engravings and appeared as nothing more than oval rocks. And yet there was life in them.

Surrounded by the thousand stones, I did three koras around the central stupa, on the third feeling the heat and sharpness of the gravelled path under my bare feet. Upon completing the third kora, words surfaced in my mind: *We are the bedrock from which new life springs forth.*

I heard myself respond, *How is what we are doing creating the bedrock from which new life springs forth?*

Our plans changed last minute. Chantal had come down with a fever and cold from our hike up Fuji-san, so we opted to skip a six-day hike along Japan's Kumano Kodō pilgrimage trail, instead using a base camp for smaller day hikes and excursions. On our final day, we visited the mountain-top temple village of Kōya-san, perhaps Japan's most sacred temple sanctuary.

It was en route to Kōya-san that I learned of a monk named Kūkai, the founder of the complex and considered by many to be Japan's greatest saint. In the ninth century, Kūkai—later known as Kōbō Daishi—brought the Buddha's most esoteric teachings (often called his secret teachings) to Japan. These teachings are said to be so obscure that they could not be understood with our conceptual languages, and hence were never written down. Kūkai, whose name means "sky and sea," became etched into Japan's culture and its people's hearts in much the same way Fuji-san is embedded into the sea and sky.

The more I read about Kūkai, the more I grew fascinated by the synchronicities of our journey. It was Kūkai who had meditated and practised in seclusion in the mountain cave of Hasedera. It was also Kūkai who founded the sacred temple of the forgotten gravestones at Adashino. And now, at the end of our journey, we were heading to Kūkai's final resting place on Kōya-san, where he is believed to be in eternal meditation.

We'd been walking in Kūkai's footsteps without even knowing who he was.

For over 1,200 years, Japan has buried its dead around Kūkai's mausoleum at Okunoin Temple. Okunoin is now an enormous graveyard, the largest in Japan. There are over two hundred thousand graves here, from feudal families to samurai to monks and countless other honoured families and individuals. And there are over 1,300 old-growth cedars towering over the gravestones, their roots pushing aside or merging with some of the monuments. Beneath the trees, the air was full. Cleansing. Alive.

Chantal and I followed the cobble-stoned path through the cemetery, listening to the many intricate sounds and whispers of the forest: the chorus of crickets, the varied calls of birds, and myriad strange sounds.

"These cedar trees are the temple," Chantal remarked as she took in her surroundings. "Why must we as humans feel the need to keep building elaborate structures and golden statues to worship? Why can't we simply be present with the trees?"

The overstorey kept the sweltering heat of the sun from penetrating the forest, creating an oxygen-abundant environment. The earth was soft and rich, fertilizing the undergrowth, giving way to more life. Dense moss draped the trees and stone and earth alike. The forest's fragrance filled our lungs like a nourishing elixir.

Elders coexisting with Elders. Life giving life. Nothing gone. All transforming.

Eventually, we crossed the third stone bridge, making our way to the end of the path where a large temple marked Kūkai's mausoleum.

We entered the shadowy chamber. Stone-solemn monks in autumn robes were seated under the luminous glow of dim light. A few visitors were dispersed near the entrance. Some standing, others sitting or kneeling. All in silent prayer.

After a while we exited the temple from a side door to the left, emerging back into the forest where more people were in prayer. We continued gently along the path behind the temple until we found ourselves alone under the great trees.

Not far down the path I was compelled to pause before a large mound of earth. The mound was adorned with stones, which appeared even older than the ones we'd seen throughout the graveyard. Weathered and faded and overgrown with moss, they almost looked as though they had grown from the earth. Unlike the other graves, the mound did not look like a burial. Rather, it resembled some sort of dwelling place. A ghostly presence emanated from it.

In the centre of the mound was an opening. More stones were carefully placed inside, though it was hard for me to make them out. As I stared deep into the mound, I began to make out a figure. The figure was me. It mimicked my every movement, as though I was gazing into a mirror. The reflection then began to fade, and through the blackness a vast universe revealed itself. Mountain and ocean, past and present, self and other, sound and silence—all became indistinct, as though a thousand worlds became like a thousand sheets of translucent paper overlaid atop each other, each merging into another until all merged into itself.

Through the dark came a voice:

Look not at my skin
Look not in my eyes
Look not at my mind.
Look into my Heart
You will lose your vision
Like mirrorless glass
at last you will see everything.

The black hole returned to being a black hole.

When we look into the world, what do we see? Is what we see not a reflection of ourselves? A reality of our own thoughts, emotions, and beliefs?

What if our practice in life is not to achieve perfection in anything but simply to come to "know our own mind as it really is."[43] To soften enough to recognize the illusion of our own reflection, just as we would look through the reflection of the moon on a still body of water and into the depthlessness beneath. To notice each passing thought as we would the slow falling of an autumn leaf, or the tranquil current of a cedar forest stream. To realize we are also the reflection of the sun and sky.

"When you understand one thing through and through," said Soto Zen monk and teacher Shunryu Suzuki, "you understand everything. When you try to understand everything, you will not understand anything. The best way is to understand yourself and then you will understand everything."[44]

So the questions are not, Can I achieve happiness? Can I achieve peace? Can I achieve enlightenment? The question is, Can I choose to practice, in every thought, in every action, in every moment of every day? "Healing is a pilgrimage," said Paula Arai.[45]

The purer our practice, the more our mind will open to the innate nature of all that is. More and more we will hear its fine chorus. We will see its grace in the world. We will feel its nourishment in our bodies. No longer lost and confused, we will live with the wisdom of Earth. Whatever may happen we will meet it with curiosity, wonder, compassion, and ease; we will find our stable ground.

How do we go across a dangerous steep ridge at ease? The same way we go through life: at ease.

Incense burns below
A spider rests in its web
Smoke passes through it

Sun, Moon, and Stars

"Are you going into the woods?"
"Yes, I am going into the woods; I am going into the unity of all things."

—Hermann Hesse (Siddhartha)

Better than one hundred years lived
    Without seeing the arising and passing of things
Is one day lived
    Seeing their arising and passing.

—The Buddha

I STOOD BEFORE THE ROCK FACE, mesmerized—my eyes exploring its detail like the surface of a painting. I'd grown accustomed to examining rocks, studying their unique features—pockets and crystals, edges and hollows, stripes and lines. Every one of them has a story, told over millions of years.

This one, however, was different. On it were scratched images unlike anything I'd seen. Some etchings were of strange human-like figures—creatures with broad shoulders and horns. Others looked as though they were frozen in some sort of ceremonial dance. There were horses and deer-like animals, some adorned with crescent-shaped horns, others with elaborate antlers nearly the size of the animal. Different foot and paw tracks were dotted about, some thin, others wide, some with claws, others with six toes. Amid it all were spirals and circles, and long curving zig-zagged lines, as though showing the map to somewhere.

Archaeologists call it a petroglyph panel—perhaps the only recorded history of the peoples at that time, some two thousand years ago. To the Diné, the rock is called Tse' Hane—rock that tells a story. I couldn't decipher their story, but it didn't matter. There was something deeply relatable about the etchings, something that whispered through the barrier of time—as though the message the carvers left behind was not meant to be understood with the eyes.

Klem and I were in the desert canyonlands of Utah and had just finished two days of climbing steep cracks and crevasses carved into sandstone formations that can only be described as artistic wonders of the world. The rust-red, castle-like towers and winding canyons took over sixty-five million years to form, and they continue to form.

It was our last day in the desert and our bodies felt battered from the climbing, so we decided to take a rest day and observe an annular solar eclipse that would occur later that morning. During this eclipse, the moon would cover all but a thin edge of the sun, creating a ring of fire in the sky. The local diners had renamed desserts and drinks for the occasion.

We pulled off onto a dirt road, as good a spot as any. We donned our peculiar-looking protective shades and, in an endless sea of sagebrush, we watched the moon creep its way in front of the midday sun.

Another car pulled up next to us and a couple jumped out. "Have we missed it? Has it happened yet?"

"It's just happening now," I replied.

The couple slipped on their rectangular glasses, and the four of us stared motionless at the sky. Bit by bit, we watched the moon pass before the sun, wreathing itself in a fiery halo. For a brief moment, Earth, moon, and sun aligned as one, before resuming their separate journeys.

"I thought it would last longer," the woman remarked, then the two of them hopped back into their vehicle and sped off down the desert highway.

Klem and I stayed for a while.

Ravens dancing
in a cerulean sky
The scent of wild sagebrush
Quiets the mind.
Desert towers
From another age
Still as statues
Marking passages of time
Into the horizon
The red canyons flow
Calling my name
To where I do not know.

How extraordinary it is—at this moment we are spinning through space, orbiting an enormous ball of fire, all in some utterly perfect and miraculous union enabling life as we know it. And yet, if we are present to it, we can witness the gift every day in plain sight.

If we can witness such a phenomenon in the sky, can we not slow ourselves enough to witness the miracle behind our own thoughts?

A few days later, I find myself sitting by a campfire in the forest behind our home in Squamish. Even though I know there are heated, well-lit rooms just a few metres away, with soft cushions to relax into, there is something comforting about being outside under the starry skies and full moon. The fire glows, warming my hands and face against the cold autumn air of the Pacific Northwest. Like the petroglyphs, the flames awaken a deep and primordial passage to an ancient story, a story before names.

Names are given. But what is a name made of? Memory and story. The bones of ancestors. Stones etched with meaning.

How many names have we carried? How many names have we chosen? How many names have been lost in time?

The warmth of the fire draws me nearer.

For too long we've observed nature at a distance, as something separate, something to control. How can we, who are born of fire, hope to tame it? How can we set it apart when it is so innately part of us?

The burning flame rises, yet I know it's not my hand that feels its heat. I witness the amber blaze, yet I know it's not my eyes that see it. I breathe in a wisp of smoke, yet I know it's not my nose that smells it. Embers hiss and crack, yet I know it's not my ears that hear them.

Real as my senses seem, they exist in my conceptual mind. And it is only because of the paper-thin time it takes for transmission that things appear otherwise. My eyes don't see, my hand does not feel, my nose does not smell, nor do my ears hear. It is but a finely crafted illusion.

In the same way, thoughts and emotions rise and fall away within me, and yet I know they are not who I am. For behind them all is another observer.[46] A subtle wakefulness. Perhaps we, like our thoughts, are symbols—markings etched in rock destined to return to the great expanse of the unborn, beyond origin and destination, just as sunlight on a body of water reflects back unto itself.

The conceptual mind becomes quiescent, said Ramana Maharshi, when we look deeply into ourselves. According to Ramana Maharshi, the repeated thought *Who am I?* eventually dissolves all other thoughts and, "like the stick used for stirring the burning pyre," it will itself be dissolved. "Then, there will arise Self-realization."[47]

What happens when we let our stories dissolve? What happens when we let go of the story of our beliefs, the story of who we think we are, even the story of our own name? What happens when we learn to abide by the sacred silence that brings us home? What happens when we learn to see behind our story, knowing we exist not as the words on the page but rather as the page on which the words are written.

In doing so, we would realize we are all manifestations of the same essence. We would realize we are our own witness, just as Earth is our witness. Our awareness would be rooted in loving kindness, equanimity, compassion, and empathetic joy.

Some names cannot be spoken, for there is no language for them.

My phone lights up and begins to buzz. It's Pemba. She's just wrapped up a Model United Nations conference at her school, where they came together with several other schools to discuss the UN's seventeen Sustainable Development Goals.

Two years ago, Pemba approached Chantal and me about pursuing her studies (and future) in Canada. "It felt right," she said, and since she was the youngest of six sisters, she felt she had the best opportunity to take care of her family. An education in Canada would give her that chance.

At thirteen years old, Pemba took it upon herself to apply for one of the top schools not far from where we live—a boarding school known for supporting youth from different countries with varying socio-economic backgrounds. Upon making it through the written application, she cruised through the Zoom interview. I will never forget one of her questions to the admissions director: "You may know at our school in Kathmandu we spend a lot of time preserving our Tibetan culture. What do you do at your school to preserve your culture?"

The school opened its arms to her.

Chantal and I had met Pemba when she was just three years old, running around her family's stone mountain home at an elevation of 4,150 metres in the high Himalaya. We couldn't speak each other's language at that time. And yet we bonded.

We'd been told Pemba was born two months premature, not breathing. With her village tucked deep in the mountains, and days from any roads, health care, and medical doctors, infant mortality ran high. Her mother had already lost two infant sons. But Pemba's family gathered around her tiny unmoving body, gently blowing life force toward her head, chest, hands, and feet—a tradition long practised in her village. Finally came the cries of a newborn baby. Pemba had beaten the odds.

Now at fifteen years old, Pemba is FaceTiming with me about the future of the world, exploring topics like ethical dimensions, climate change, and social equity. She's excited to share her experience.

"Traditional values and rituals could be upheld," Pemba had advocated with her group, "as long as they don't harm or create inequality for women."

She reminds me of something the Buddha once taught about wisdom and compassion—how these two seemingly separate forces coexist to create a natural harmony on Earth. Wisdom, according to Buddhism, is the ability to see reality as it is. The ability to discern Truth. Compassion is the ability to act with *upaya-kausalya*, or "skillful means."

Just as the biodiversity of a forest works together to support and give life to itself, a symmetry of wisdom and compassion is fundamental to our existence. Wisdom requires the right—or awakened—action, which requires wisdom. There is no duality with wisdom and compassion, for without one the other cannot exist.

In Tibetan Buddhism, wisdom is represented by the sacred feminine. Compassion is represented by the masculine. Each of us is born with both. More and more, however, wherever we look we witness biodiversity out of balance. Life out of balance. For too long there has been a widespread suppression of the sacred feminine—in women, in men, and in our collective relationship with Mother Earth.

"The warm is getting warmer," Pemba's father once shared with me about his village. "The cold is getting colder. When it rains, there is more rain. When it doesn't rain, there is less."

Of all the female deities in the Tibetan Buddhist pantheon there is one who is revered more than all others: Tara, whose name in Sanskrit means "star." She is an ageless light. Like the rising sun, she guides us from darkness. She gives us warmth. She gives us life. She is referred to as the "Embodiment of Perfected Wisdom, the Goddess of Universal Compassion, and the Mother of all Buddhas."[48]

Tara is a physical manifestation of the sacred feminine. When we invoke her power, we awaken a sacred wisdom from which we were born. This power endows us with the courage to be vulnerable, to forgive, to be at peace. To see Truth and live with compassion and equanimity. This sacred wisdom of the Heart transcends reason and concept.

The way to Tara is not through thought or logic, nor clamour or effort. The way is to find stillness. To listen. To breathe as though each breath is a part of the forest. She may appear when we least expect it. On a mountain or among the trees. In a cave or in the flames of a campfire, or when we feel afraid, lost, or confused. She may even appear as a vision, or as a soft whisper while we're asleep. Or in the eyes of a child.

When she appears, keep her close. Trust in her, for she never left us. Honour her. She is our path to liberation, ever guiding us to transform our deepest hurt into wisdom.

The fire's embers pulse gently as its flames begin to soften. Pemba and I remain on FaceTime together in silence—Pemba in her dorm room, me under the night sky, both of us watching the full moon and stars travel across the sky for a while.

I'm reminded of a quotation by Antoine de Saint-Exupéry: "Life has taught us that love does not consist in gazing at each other, but in looking outward together in the same direction."[49]

"In your village, do people spend a lot of time gazing at the stars—tracking them?" I ask Pemba.

"What do you mean?" she replies.

"Well, looking at the constellations, figuring out their patterns. Coming up with stories about them?"

"To us they are just stars. But we do depend on them for the weather—like if there are a lot of stars out, we know the night will be cold and the sky will be clear tomorrow. We also use the light of the moon and stars as our 'streetlights.'"

"I like that," I say. "They're just stars, helping us find our way."

"Mikari, are you Buddhist?" Pemba asks. Her question catches me a bit by surprise. Ever since she was a kid, she's had a knack for springing these kinds of questions on me.

"Are *you* Buddhist?" I reply.

"It's something in our culture. Something I have always been."

I pause for a moment.

"Well...for me it's a good question," I say. "The Buddha was not Buddhist. Just as Jesus wasn't Christian. I practise Buddhist teachings, but I don't consider myself anything. I suppose I just *am*. I do like what the fourteenth Dalai Lama said: 'My religion is very simple. My religion is kindness.'"

Pemba smiles in agreement.

"What does being Buddhist mean to you?" I ask.

"To me, being Buddhist means to be myself."

I hear myself respond with the words of Shakespeare: "This above all: to thine own self be true."

Though we may be made of a million stories, we are all expressions of one Truth.

The hour is getting late, and it is time for Pemba to go to bed. Soon the light of the stars will fade, the moon will turn, and the sun will rise.

"What is Truth?" asked the voice.

"All happens as it is, and that is All," it answered.

Acknowledgements

Every literary creation is the collective work of many minds and hearts.

I'd like to offer a heartfelt thank you to my early readers and fellow Sangha members Tony Humphries, Sara Daly, Brian Finnie, and Shirley Blair for your support, guidance, and the wisdom you generously shared with me.

To kindred spirit and friend Paula Arai—*arigato gozaimasu*, and a deep bow.

I'd also like to extend my sincere gratitude to Stephanie Tade, Beth Grossman, Kirsten Craven, and Ruth Wilson. And to Amanda Lewis—the best editor I could have hoped for—who helped turn small steps into a completed journey.

Thank you to Jaz for infusing your creative genius into these pages, and to the whole Hohm Press family—Bala, Dasya, and Peter—for welcoming me in and for your care and commitment in bringing this book to light.

I'd also like to thank Andre Caron, James Frystak, and Taylor Kagel for listening to hours of ideas and musings across the course of our many mountain adventures.

To my mom and dad and sister Marita—thank you for your everlasting support, encouragement, and love. And to Junu, Karma, and Pemba—thank you for always inspiring me to keep climbing, and reminding me that the best views are the ones we share together.

My deepest gratitude goes to my wife and partner in adventure, Chantal—for every mountain shared, in both the storm and the stillness, thank you for being my grounding force, and being with me every step of the way.

And finally, to you, the reader—without whom these words would have no home. Many blessings. May you find peace and joy.

Endnotes

1 Lily Rothman, "Margaret Atwood on Serial Fiction and the Future of the Book," *Time*, October 8, 2012, https://entertainment.time.com/2012/10/08/margaret-atwood-on-serial-fiction-and-the-future-of-the-book/.

2 Alison Gopnik, *The Philosophical Baby: What Children's Minds Tell Us about Truth, Love, and the Meaning of Life* (Farrar, Straus and Giroux, 2009).

3 James Lovelock, Foreword, *Earthy Realism: The Meaning of Gaia*, ed. Mary Midgley (Societas, 2014), 2.

4 James Lovelock, *Gaia: A New look at Life on Earth* (Oxford University Press, 2016), 9.

5 Tyler Dewar, "What Is Tendrel?" Lions Roar, https://www.lionsroar.com/tendrel/.

6 Ken Wilber, *Eye to Eye: The Quest for the New Paradigm* (Shambhala, 2001), 252.

7 Chögyam Trungpa Rinpoche, *Shambhala: The Sacred Path of the Warrior* (Shambhala, 1984), 114.

8 Andrew Olendzki, "What's in a Word? Prajñā," *Tricycle: The Buddhist Review*, 2021, https://tricycle.org/magazine/prajna-meaning/.

9 Wilber, *Eye to Eye*, 17.

10 Jared Diamond, *The World Until Yesterday: What Can We Learn from Traditional Societies?* (Viking, 2012).

11 Gabor Maté, *The Myth of Normal: Trauma, Illness and Healing in a Toxic Culture* (Knopf Canada, 2022), 51.

12 Carl G. Jung, *Man and His Symbols* (Aldus Books, 1964), 85.

13 Lawrence E. Joseph, "James Lovelock, Gaia's Grand Old Man," *Salon*, August 17, 2000, https://www.salon.com/2000/08/17/lovelock/.

14 Hermann Hesse, *Demian* (Start Publishing LLC, 2015), 103.

15 Chögyam Trungpa Rinpoche, Commentary, *The Tibetan Book of the Dead* (Shambhala, 2019), 18.

16 Alexandre Dumas, *The Count of Monte Cristo* (Collins, 1986), 1094.

17 Chögyam Trungpa, *Milarepa: Lessons from the Life & Songs of Tibet's Great Yogi* (Shambhala, 2017), 56.

18 PBS Nova Documentary, *Secrets of the Sky Tomb*, Season 44, Episode 1 (2018).

19 Charles Ramble, "Trouble with Vampires: or, How the Layout of This Book Came to be Done," *Tibetan and Himalayan Healing: An Anthology for Anthony Aris* (Vajra Books, 2015), 571.

20 This is also the English translation of the title to Levi's book, *Il futuro ha un cuore antico* (Einaudi, 2025).

21 Maté, *The Myth of Normal*, 186.

22 Gil Fronsdal, *The Dhammapada* (Shambhala, 2005), 4.

23 Rupert Gethin, *The Foundations of Buddhism* (Oxford University Press, 1998), 27.

24 Gethin, *The Foundations of Buddhism*, 35.

25 Gethin, *The Foundations of Buddhism*, 35.

26 Gethin, *The Foundations of Buddhism*, 72.

27 René Daumal, *Mount Analogue* (The Overlook Press, 2004), 104.

28 Alison Mayes, "Look to the Medicine Wheel for Mental Health, Elders Advise in First Nations Study," *UM Today News*, January 30, 2019, https://news.umanitoba.ca/look-to-the-medicine-wheel-for-mental-health-elders-advise-in-first-nations-study/.

29 Joseph Polimeni, "The Shamanistic Theory of Schizophrenia: The Evidence for Schizophrenia as a Vestigial Phenotypic Behavior Originating in Paleolithic Shamanism," *Journal of Anthropological and Archaeological Sciences* 6, no. 3 (2022), chrome-extension://efaidnbmnnnibpcajpcglclefindmkaj/https://lupinepublishers.com/anthropological-and-archaeological-sciences/pdf/JAAS.MS.ID.000238.pdf.

30 Joseph Campbell, "Dr. Joseph Campbell—Inward Journey: Schizophrenia and Mythology," *The* NYPR *Archive Collections*, 1969, https://www.wnyc.org/story/dr-joseph-campbell-inward-journey-schizophrenia-and-mythology/.

31 Joseph Campbell, *The Hero with a Thousand Faces* (New World Library, 2008), 333.

32 Peter Matthiessen, *The Snow Leopard* (Penguin, 2008), 208.

33 Jane Austen, *Pride and Prejudice*, Chapter 27, Project Gutenberg ebook, https://www.gutenberg.org/cache/epub/1342/pg1342-images.html#CHAPTER_XXVII.

34 John Krakauer, *Eiger Dreams: Ventures among Men and Mountains* (Doubleday, 1990), 181.

35 Laurence Gonzales, *Deep Survival: Who Lives, Who Dies, and Why* (W.W. Norton, 2017), 49.

36 Referencing philosopher and psychologist William James's theory of emotion.

37 Trungpa Rinpoche, *Shambhala*, 56.

38 Thich Nhat Hanh, *Touching Peace: Practicing the Art of Mindful Living* (Parallax Press, 2005), 8.

39 Matthiessen, *The Snow Leopard*, 208.

40 Miyamoto Musashi, *The Book of Five Rings* (Shambhala, 2002), xxxii.

41 Walter Bonatti, *The Mountains of My Life* (Penguin, 2010), 252.

42 Paula Arai, *Painting Enlightenment: Healing Visions of the Heart Sutra* (Shambhala, 2019), 102.

43 Kūkai, as quoted in Yoshito S. Hakeda, trans., *Kūkai: Major Works* (Columbia University Press, 1984), 68.

44 Shunryu Suzuki, *Zen Mind, Beginner's Mind: Informal Talks on Zen Meditation and Practice* (Shambhala, 2020), 101.

45 Paula Arai, *The Little Book of Zen Healing* (Shambhala, 2023), 185.

46 Often referred to as *saakshi* (Sanskrit), "the silent witness."

47 Ramana Maharshi, *Who Am I? (Nan Yar?): The Teachings of Bhagavan Sri Ramana Maharshi* (Wisdom Books, 2024), 9.

48 Meher McArthur, "Tara: A Powerful Feminine Force in the Buddhist Pantheon," March 20, 2019, Buddhistdoor Global, https://www.buddhistdoor.net/features/tara-a-powerful-feminine-force-in-the-buddhist-pantheon/.

49 Antoine de Saint-Exupéry, *Wind, Sand and Stars* (Mariner Books Classics, 2010), 169.

Photo: Alison Wandzura

MICHAEL SCHAUCH is an alpinist and award-winning author who lives to explore the depths of nature and the human spirit and share the beauty of connection he discovers along the way.

For fifteen years Michael has been a mentor and supporter of Tibetan Buddhist youth in Kathmandu, Nepal, and many young members of his community in Canada. He holds an MBA from Queens University and is a member of the Explorers Club.

He and his wife Chantal make their base camp in the traditional, ancestral, and unceded territory of the Sḵwx̱wú7mesh Nation (Squamish, BC), nestled in the rugged Coast Mountains and temperate rainforests of the Pacific Northwest.

To learn more, visit www.michaelschauch.com.